Laurence B. Siegel
The Ford Foundation

Benchmarks and Investment Management

The Research Foundation of AIMR™

Research Foundation Publications

Benchmarks and Investment Management

ISBN 0-943205-63-8

Printed in the United States of America

August 1, 2003

Editorial Staff
Bette A. Collins
Book Editor

Rebecca L. Bowman
Assistant Editor

Jaynee M. Dudley
Production Manager

Kelly T. Bruton/Lois A. Carrier
Production and Composition

Kara H. Morris
Online Production

Mission

The Research Foundation's mission is to encourage education for investment practitioners worldwide and to fund, publish, and distribute relevant research.

Biography

Laurence B. Siegel is director of investment policy research at the Ford Foundation in New York City, where he has worked since 1994. Previously, he was a managing director of Ibbotson Associates, an investment consulting firm that he helped establish in 1979. Mr. Siegel chairs the investment committee of the Trust for Civil Society in Central and Eastern Europe and serves on the investment committee of the NAACP Legal Defense Fund. He advises the boards or investment committees of numerous other organizations and was a trustee of Oberweis Emerging Growth Fund. Mr. Siegel is a member of the editorial boards of the *Journal of Portfolio Management,* Research Foundation of AIMR, and *Journal of Investing*; was the founding editor of *Investment Policy Magazine*; and is a member of the program committee of the Institute for Quantitative Research in Finance (the Q Group). He received his B.A. in urban studies from the University of Chicago in 1975 and his M.B.A. in finance from the same institution in 1977.

Contents

Acknowledgments

This book is dedicated to Connie and to Peter Bernstein.

I want to thank Linda Strumpf of the Ford Foundation for the personal and professional support that made this monograph possible. Linda, and Clinton Stevenson (also of the Ford Foundation), have taught me the plan sponsor's trade over the past eight years and have made innumerable suggestions for improving the book's contents and readability. I am also grateful to Mark Kritzman, who suggested the topic of the monograph and provided encouragement and feedback throughout the process of writing it.

This book reflects much prior work done jointly with my frequent co-author Barton Waring and also the highly productive, ongoing dialogue in which we openly share results from our separate research interests. He is effectively an unnamed co-author of Chapters 2 and 3, on active management relative to benchmarks and on building optimal portfolios of managers, respectively; and of the section in Chapter 12 on asset-allocation policy relative to the liabilities of an investment program. Indeed, the whole book benefited from his influence.

Theodore Aronson, Barclay Douglas, Arnold Wood, and Jason Zweig added much wisdom, humor, and encouragement, as well as substantive commentary in interviews and discussions. Elizabeth Hilpman provided a perspective on the investment business and the people who make it work that is an education in itself and that is vigorously reflected here. Finally, in addition to being a great friend, Peter Bernstein has set a standard of quality in writing that all essayists, whether on investment issues or in other fields, would do well to emulate.

I also wish to thank numerous other people who provided suggestions, feedback, interviews, data, and other resources. They include (in alphabetical order) Clifford Asness, Mark Carhart, Thomas Coleman, Donald Galligan, William Goetzmann, Roger Ibbotson, Stephen Johnson, David Kabiller, Paul Kaplan, Susan Ollila, Thomas Philips, Brad Pope, Thomas Schneeweis, Steven Schoenfeld, Rex Sinquefield, Mark Sladkus, and Ronald Surz. Those whom I've forgotten to thank have my apologies in advance.

In addition to these personal acknowledgements, I am grateful to the Research Foundation of AIMR for financial support for the research and writing of this monograph.

L.B.S.
Wilmette, Illinois
June 2003

Foreword

Benchmarks determine the performance of investment managers perhaps more than any other influence, including managers' determination to succeed and the resources and skills they bring to this task. We in the industry have largely overlooked this fact, perhaps at our peril. With this outstanding Research Foundation monograph, Laurence Siegel shines a bright light on the role of benchmarks, and he raises critical issues that we can no longer ignore.

Siegel begins by providing historical perspective to the topic, tracing the evolution of benchmarks from their 1884 origin with Charles Henry Dow's average of 11 railroad stocks to their alleged role in the recent stock market bubble. Along the way, he adeptly intertwines the development and application of benchmarks with the development and gradual acceptance of modern portfolio theory. He demonstrates clearly that benchmarks are the practical corollary of the efficient market hypothesis and the capital asset pricing model.

Siegel focuses much of his efforts on describing the three purposes of benchmarks:

- to function as portfolios for investors who want passive exposure to a particular market segment,
- to serve as performance standards against which to measure the contribution of active managers, and
- to act as proxies for asset classes in the formation of policy portfolios.

Although these purposes may seem self-evident once they are suggested, Siegel delves into a variety of nuances, complexities, and controversies that I suspect most readers will not have considered previously, including the features that distinguish good benchmarks from those that are inadequate.

The message that emerges throughout this monograph is the intense focus that we place on relative performance and the implication of this focus for the allocation of capital resources. For example, the reluctance of managers to depart significantly from benchmarks has the unintended consequence of channeling capital away from securities as they decline in value and toward securities as they grow in value, a practice that some believe contributes to market bubbles. It is within this context that Siegel connects benchmarks to behavioral finance.

The intense focus on benchmarks has another unintended consequence, which I alluded to previously. Together with an inadequate appreciation of within-horizon risk, the concentration on benchmarks leads managers to select securities from a narrower opportunity set than exists naturally in the capital markets—a practice that may harm both providers and users of capital.

These problems demand our attention, and this excellent monograph will help ensure that they get it. The Research Foundation is, therefore, especially pleased to present *Benchmarks and Investment Management*.

Mark Kritzman, CFA
Research Director
The Research Foundation of the
Association for Investment Management and Research

Preface

In geodetics, a benchmark is a plaque embedded in rock or soil to show the precise latitude, longitude, and altitude of a given location. That the term "benchmark" has been extended, as metaphor, to refer to standards of performance in corporate management and engineering is an intelligent and creative use of language; thus, a 95 percent on-time arrival record might be regarded as a benchmark of good performance for an airline.

But it is in the investment field that benchmarks have acquired a truly special place. Yes, in one sense, they are like benchmarks in corporate management and engineering—that is, benchmarks are paper portfolios constructed for comparison with real portfolios to see whether the latter are being managed effectively. In another sense, however, if the benchmarks are well constructed, they represent much more. They embody the opportunity set of investments in an asset class. The return on the benchmark is the return available from that asset class and from index funds of that asset class. Finally, the benchmark return is also the return (before costs) on the aggregation of all active managers who participate in the asset class. That is a lot of work for a benchmark to do.

Because of the multifaceted role of benchmarks in investing, a clear understanding of the issues surrounding benchmark construction, choice, and use is important. To begin to uncover these issues is the goal of this monograph.

To managers with real skill, benchmarks seem like shackles. "You can't live with them," such managers think, "because they tell you to buy stocks in proportion to the stocks' market capitalizations—which means, all too often, buying the stocks that have become the most overpriced." If active managers don't buy such stocks, they are accused of taking "too much" risk, too much tracking error relative to the benchmark. Such an accusation is ironic because the managers think they are *avoiding* risk by not buying overpriced securities.

To more typical managers, however—those without the ability to consistently add alpha (active return)—benchmarks are a godsend. Such managers, it seems, can't live *without* benchmarks. Benchmarks provide a starting point for portfolio holdings, a list of securities and weights that the manager should or would hold in the absence of a view on any given security. By serving as the starting point, benchmarks are also the control mechanism for active risk. Finally, investing in the benchmark provides the asset-class return, which in rising markets is often enough to satisfy the customer even if no alpha is generated.

Plan sponsors and consultants also can't live without benchmarks. Peter Bernstein has written, "Performance measurers seek benchmarks the way bees seek honey" (2000, p. 1). When charged with the responsibility of measuring something, a manager's natural response is to go out and obtain an objective, widely recognized measuring device. Whatever their flaws, benchmarks serve this role.

There is a tension between managers, who typically believe they have real skill and who bristle at the need to be measured by benchmarks, and investors, whose proper and fitting response is, "I'm from Missouri, and you've got to show me." The tension is natural and is not the fault of benchmarks. It is what happens between the seller and buyer of anything when information is incomplete or costly.

This monograph is an exploration of the many issues surrounding investment benchmarks and benchmarking. The first half of the monograph addresses the questions: What are benchmarks? What are they for? Where did they come from? Where are they going? In Chapter 1, I introduce some of the basic issues surrounding benchmarks, with a focus on U.S. equity benchmarks because they are familiar to most readers. Chapter 2 indicates how benchmarks should be used to measure performance—to isolate the "pure active return" and "pure active risk" that remain after you have adjusted for market and other factor exposures. Chapter 3 takes a brief detour to indicate how the pure active returns and risks of active managers frame an optimization problem that allows the investor to build portfolios of active managers just as he or she would, more conventionally, use similar information to build portfolios of stocks.

Chapter 4 opens with a description of the "original paradigm" that governed thinking about investing (and performance measurement) before the great discoveries of the 1950s and 1960s that led to the body of knowledge now generally referred to as modern portfolio theory. I then introduce MPT and make the natural connection between it and benchmarks. The "crisis" in portfolio theory that, arguably, culminated in the stock price bubble of 1998–2000 and the implications of that crisis for benchmarks and benchmarking are the topics of Chapter 5. In Chapter 6, I summarize the critiques of investment benchmarks and outline a compromise that might ease the tension between critics who believe that benchmarks are shackles and those who believe they are an appropriate starting point for portfolio construction, as well as the only acceptable way to measure performance. Chapter 7 discusses the impact of benchmarking on markets and institutions; I describe work that has been done to identify this impact at the micro level (in the pricing of individual securities) and in the macro sphere (in distorting market levels).

The second half of the monograph considers benchmarks as they relate to specific asset classes. Chapter 8 focuses on U.S. equity style benchmarks—first, by addressing the history and concepts surrounding them and, second, by indicating how each of the major suites of style benchmarks is constructed and revealing what trade-offs are involved in deciding how to classify stocks into styles. Chapter 9 discusses fixed-income benchmarks and makes note of two special issues surrounding them—first, that the duration of the benchmark doesn't necessarily match the duration requirements of any given investor and, second, that lower-quality bonds tend to have large weights in a benchmark. Chapter 10 deals with international equity benchmarks from the standpoint of U.S. investors. In Chapter 11, I introduce the concept of benchmarks for hedge funds. Funds that hedge are not new, but this old strategy—now revived and converted to the "new new thing"—is increasingly a part of mainstream investors' portfolios and cries out for measurement. Chapter 12 concludes the monograph by discussing *policy benchmarks*, the indexes-of-indexes used to measure how an investor's whole portfolio is doing.

Some omissions in this monograph may stand out. A book on benchmarks might be expected to contain a great deal of data, including construction rules, holdings, performance statistics, and so forth, for various competing benchmarks. Such data presentations tend not only to be voluminous, however, but also quickly become out-of-date, so I keep the data to a minimum and, instead, refer readers to other sources for detail.

Benchmarks for real estate or private equity are not discussed here, and the coverage of fixed-income benchmarks is brief and focused on a few controversial issues; those topics are not my area of comparative advantage. This book is not intended to be an encyclopedia.

Finally, I occasionally adopt a personal tone in communicating with the reader. I hope this choice turns out to be helpful without being overdone.

L.B.S.
Wilmette, Illinois
June 2003

1. Origins, Uses, and Characteristics of U.S. Equity Benchmarks

The effort to measure the performance of stock markets, as opposed to individual securities, is at least as old as Charles Henry Dow's pioneering average, which he began to calculate in 1884. The first Dow Jones average was simply the average of the prices of 11 railroad stocks. This number was published daily, providing investors with a constantly updated barometer of the market. Maybe the modern mind reads too much into the historical record, but it is tempting to conclude that the construction and popularity of this early market index reflected an awareness that trends in "the market" had a bearing on the prices of individual issues, not just the other way around.[1]

Between 1885 and today, by far the most important innovation in index construction was that made by the Standard Securities Corporation (now Standard & Poor's), which in 1923 constructed the first market-capitalization-weighted index. This index, a composite of 223 securities, later evolved into the S&P 500 Index. Such an index gives each company a weight in proportion to the total market value of that company's outstanding shares. Most of the market indexes in use today, and all those covered in this study, are market-cap weighted. (The Dow Jones Industrial Average, DJIA, in contrast, implicitly weights each company by its per share stock price; other weighting schemes, such as equal weighting, are found in a few other indexes.) The principle of market-cap weighting is so central to modern index construction that I treat it in a separate section.

Today, thousands of market indexes, representing every conceivable country, asset class, and investment style, are available. And although this abundance reflects the explosive growth of the investment industry and suggests a healthy emphasis on quantifying investment results and processes, it also makes differentiation among the many indexes difficult.[2]

---

[1]This chapter initially appeared in a modified form in Enderle, Pope, and Siegel (2002, 2003), which focused not on benchmarks (indexes) in general but on broad-capitalization indexes of equities in the United States. By "broad capitalization," we meant indexes that include stocks of all market sizes—large, medium, and small—as opposed to specialized indexes that measure stocks in only one size category.

[2]Throughout this monograph, I use "benchmark" as a synonym for "index" when the index is being used as a point of comparison for actual portfolios.

Uses of Benchmarks

Over the years, the use of benchmarks has expanded far beyond their original role as a general indicator of market sentiment and direction. They have become central to investment management, with an impact on active management, asset allocation, and performance measurement and reward as well as passive indexing.

"How's the Market?"—Gauge of Sentiment. From the beginning, market indexes have been widely used to answer the question: What is happening in the investment world at this minute? As early users of the DJIA could appreciate, reducing the prices of diverse securities in a market to a single statistic is useful because it reveals the net effect of all factors at work in a market. These factors include not only hopes and fears specific to companies in the index but also broader factors—war, peace, economic expansion, recession, and so forth—that can potentially affect share values. Thus, a frequently updated domestic stock market index gives an indication of how well your home country is thriving at a given point in time.

The use of an index as a sentiment indicator is particularly notable in times of stress, such as when the Allies were faring poorly in World War II (stock indexes were extremely depressed) and when President John F. Kennedy was assassinated (after the large one-day decline, a strong rebound was taken as a sign that national confidence had not been destroyed).

Triple Duty. Market indexes have developed many disparate uses. Because they have market-cap weighting as a characteristic in common, essentially all of the benchmarks of a given market (or market subset) give approximately the same indication of that market's general trends. The principal uses of indexes that motivate us to distinguish one index from another are

* as portfolios (index funds),
* as benchmarks for actively managed funds, and
* as proxies for asset classes in asset allocation.

Practically all benchmarks or indexes are called upon to perform all these tasks, and more. So, when evaluating or trying to understand an index, you must consider the suitability of that index from the point of view of all three of these principal uses.

■ *Portfolios (index funds).* With the growing understanding of portfolio theory, which suggests that beating the market on a risk-adjusted basis is difficult, market-cap-weighted indexes turned out to be preadapted to an important and revolutionary new use—index funds. By simply matching the holdings of a well-constructed index, a portfolio manager can provide the return on the index, minus expenses (which tend to be very low for index funds). In the long run, this asset-class return, rather than value added through stock-selection skill, forms the majority of the gain from investing. Index fund management has become a big business.

An index for which an index fund cannot be constructed is generally not a good index. An example is the Value Line composite, which is calculated by taking the geometric mean of the constituent returns. Because no one can earn this rate of return, the index has limited usefulness. Similarly, equally weighted indexes are flawed as far as indexing is concerned because an index fund designed to track such an index would require constant rebalancing, as a result of stock price changes. Also, it would have limited capacity because the smallest stocks in such an index would quickly become scarce as investors bought into the strategy.

Cap-weighted indexes, in contrast, are excellent bases for index funds, as is noted in detail later in this chapter.

■ *Starting point for active management.* Many active investors—particularly quantitative, active managers of risk-controlled, enhanced-index portfolios—use the contents of an index as their starting point and deviate from index weights according to the degree of conviction they have that a particular stock is more or less attractive than the market as a whole.

Practically all active managers, however—not only those who use the benchmark as a starting point for selecting the portfolio but also traditional active managers—use benchmarks for performance measurement and evaluation and for assessing how much "active risk" they are taking. The investment management consulting industry has cooperated with academics and plan sponsors in making clear the distinction between *policy risk*, the risk that comes from holding the benchmark itself, and *active risk*, the risk that is represented by deviations (resulting from active management) from the benchmark holdings. Chapter 2 covers this distinction, and Chapter 3 explores the logical consequences of adopting this way of looking at the world.

As a result of active managers and investors using benchmarks as starting points and measuring tools, the term "risk" has become closely identified with tracking error (deviation from the benchmark). To explore this connection is one of the central purposes of this monograph. At least until the great bear market of 2000–2003, the profound importance of policy risk tended to be neglected as investors focused their attention on active risk—tracking error—as the real risk that needed to be managed in a portfolio. In Chapter 2, I argue that achieving active return while avoiding active risk is the only goal active managers should pursue *but only after* the greater questions—what policy risks to take and how much of each—have already been decided by the investor.

■ *Asset-class proxies.* Finally, as asset allocation has come to the forefront of the practice of investing, analysts have studied the historical returns and other characteristics of indexes in an attempt to understand the behavior of the asset classes they represent. A benchmark constructed on a consistent basis across time allows you to calculate long-run rates of return and to compare market levels at points widely separated in time.

In addition, investors can use benchmarks to compare the risks of various asset classes and to measure the changes in risk of a given asset class over time, to calculate correlations and gains from diversification among asset classes, and to perform other analyses relevant to determining investment policy.

Performance Measurement, Risk Analysis, and Fee Calculation. One of the pleasing—and possibly unintended—consequences of having a market index available is that it answers the question: Did I beat the market? From the time indexes began to be constructed, the natural human desire to best one's competitors surely must have motivated investors to compare their portfolio returns with index returns. The founding of an organized investment management profession in the 1920s spurred the development of methods to make this comparison more accurate. Today, the modern science of performance measurement, evaluation, and attribution draws on the academic achievements of the 1960s—the capital asset pricing model (CAPM) and related work—in using statistical measures to determine to what extent, and why, a particular portfolio beat or was beaten by a market index.

As noted in the Preface, a "benchmark" in ordinary English is a standard of performance, usually of good or at least acceptable performance, used as a point of comparison. This language has been extended to investment management in a precise way: The benchmark for portfolio performance is the total return on a (usually) cap-weighted index of the securities in the asset class, or subclass, in which the portfolio is intended to be invested. A cap-weighted index is usually used because it is the most workable basis for an index fund of the asset class (or subclass) that could be held as a low-cost, passive alternative to the active strategy being measured. In addition, if the CAPM is correct, a cap-weighted benchmark is efficient, in the sense of having the highest expected return at a given level of risk (volatility).

As a corollary to the use of benchmarks to measure active return, benchmarks are also used to set performance fees—fees that are a proportion of the value added by the active manager beyond the return available from merely buying the benchmark. Clearly, if performance measurement is to be carried out and performance fees are to be set fairly, the benchmark needs to be both well constructed and appropriate to the portfolio being measured.

The story behind the way in which indexes became benchmarks is documented in Chapter 4.

Characteristics of a Good Benchmark

For an index to serve as a useful benchmark, it must have certain characteristics, the most important of which is market-cap weighting.

Weighting. For several vitally important reasons, market-cap weighting is the central organizing principle of good index construction. The first and simplest reason is macro consistency: As noted previously, if everyone held a market-cap-weighted index fund and there were no active investors, all stocks would be held with none left over. With other weighting schemes, it is mathematically impossible for all investors to hold the index.

Second, market-cap weighting is the only weighting scheme consistent with a buy-and-hold strategy: The manager of a full-replication fund needs to trade only to reinvest dividends, to keep pace with changes in the index constituents, and to reflect modifications in index weights caused by changes in the constituent companies' numbers of shares outstanding.[3] In contrast, indexes that are not cap weighted require constant rebalancing because of ordinary changes in the prices of stocks.

Third, as explained in Chapter 4, according to the CAPM, the cap-weighted market index is the only portfolio of risky assets that is mean–variance efficient. That is, no portfolio can be constructed with the same risk and a higher expected return or with the same expected return and lower risk. If CAPM conditions hold, all investors should hold only this portfolio plus or minus positions in the riskless asset (because each investor must be able to choose his or her desired risk level). Of course, the stringent conditions under which the CAPM was derived don't actually hold, and investors deviate from the index for many valid reasons, including the desire to boost returns through active management. Because of the special place that a cap-weighted index holds in capital market theory, however, such an index is a good baseline.

To represent the shares available for purchase by the public better than a pure market-cap-weighted index can, some index constructors remove closely held and illiquid shares for the purpose of calculating a company's number of shares outstanding. In general, such "float adjustment" increases an index's usefulness as a benchmark, and as the basis for an index fund, because portfolio

---

[3]A full-replication fund holds every security in the index in proportion to its index weight; an optimized or sampled fund, which attempts to track an index using a subset of the securities in the index, may require more frequent rebalancing even if the fund is based on a cap-weighted index.

managers cannot typically buy shares held by founders, directors, employees, other corporations, and governmental bodies.[4] But although float adjustment, which is treated in detail in Chapter 10 in the discussion of international equity benchmarks, conveys substantial advantages to an index, it should not be considered a prerequisite of a well-constructed benchmark.

Other Characteristics. Ideally, the best choice of an index is one that, simultaneously, is useful as a benchmark for active management, can be used as the basis for index funds, and can provide proxies for asset classes in asset allocation. When selecting an index to use for one or more of these purposes, you must consider all the characteristics of the index and determine the fit with your needs. No benchmark is perfect, so (as with most choices) trade-offs are involved.

How should you choose among the competing alternatives? In addition to market-cap weighting, which is a literal prerequisite of a good index and which is common to all indexes covered here, at least seven criteria are useful in identifying a good benchmark:

1. completeness,
2. investability,
3. clear, published rules and open governance structure,
4. accurate and complete data,
5. acceptance by investors,
6. availability of crossing opportunities, derivatives, and other tradable products, and
7. low turnover and related transaction costs.

Note that these criteria are best applied when choosing a benchmark for U.S. equities or for a size or style subset of the U.S. equity market; for other asset classes and for international equities, satisfying all these requirements is more difficult. **Table 1.1** summarizes the characteristics of the principal broad-cap benchmarks of the U.S. equity market, including the S&P 500 and the Russell 1000 Index (which are often used as broad-cap benchmarks even though they are really large-cap indexes). To provide a framework by which investors can choose a benchmark, Enderle, Pope, and Siegel (2003) rated the benchmarks in Table 1.1 according to each of the seven criteria listed here. U.S. equity style benchmarks are covered in a similar manner in Chapter 8, and international equity benchmarks are covered in Chapter 10.

---

[4] Governmental holding of corporate equities is a major consideration in many non-U.S. markets but not in the U.S. market.

Table 1.1. Characteristics of Broad-Cap Indexes of the U.S. Equity Market, 31 December 2002
($ in thousands)

Statistic	Wilshire 5000	Russell 3000	Dow Jones Total Market	S&P 1500	Russell 1000	S&P 500
Capitalization data						
Number of stocks	5,637	2,955	1,579	1,500	991	500
Total market cap ($)	10,160,084,866	8,989,393,568	8,865,970,840	9,135,504,640	8,389,336,332	8,107,401,639
Cap of largest company ($)	276,411,465	241,984,724	242,269,619	276,411,465	241,984,724	276,411,465
Cap of smallest company ($)	48	3,790	61,245	39,165	120,150	279,286
Weighted-average market cap ($)	62,747,682	61,148,735	61,699,861	68,299,843	65,485,068	76,709,263
Fundamental characteristics						
Dividend yield	1.71%	1.82%	1.80%	1.73%	1.84%	1.81%
Beta	1.00	1.00	1.02	0.99	1.01	0.99
Price/book ratio	2.286	2.361	2.38	2.465	2.467	2.559
Price/earnings ratio	23.6	22.7	23.0	22.6	21.9	22.4
Inception date for historical data	January 1971	January 1979	January 1992	January 1995	January 1979	January 1926

Notes: Russell and Dow Jones numbers reflect float-adjusted market cap. Beta is relative to the S&P 500 over the 60 months ended 31 December 2002. S&P 500 data start March 1957 and have been linked by Ibbotson Associates (2003) with a predecessor index, the S&P 90, to form a continuous series from 1926 to the present.

Source: Data from Enderle, Pope, and Siegel (2003).

Trade-Offs in Benchmark Construction and Selection

In this section, I discuss the principal trade-offs involved in building and maintaining broad-cap indexes of the U.S. equity market. Style, fixed-income, and international indexes involve specialized trade-offs, some of which are discussed in the chapters that pertain to those asset classes.

Completeness vs. Investability. From a purely theoretical standpoint, the ideal index includes every security in its asset class. No one knows exactly how many stocks are in the United States, but the Wilshire 5000 (so named because it was originally composed of 5,000 stocks) contained 5,637 stocks as of 31 December 2002 and thus included more issues than any other widely distributed U.S. equity index. Many of the small-cap stocks in the Wilshire 5000 are illiquid, however, so investors would have a difficult time trading them. No full-replication index fund has ever been constructed for the Wilshire 5000.[5]

For this reason, a somewhat less broad index is more investable and accessible. By "investable," I mean that the stocks in the index can be bought and sold by a fund manager in sufficient volume that a full-replication index fund or one that is nearly full replication can be constructed without incurring high transaction costs or unusual delays because of illiquidity of index constituents. A particular index is accessible to investors to the extent that the index is the basis for existing index funds and exchange-traded funds (ETFs).[6] Access to the index through derivatives (futures and options) is desirable but less important than access through index funds and ETFs.

The Russell 3000 Index specifically excludes the smallest and most illiquid issues, so all or nearly all of its capitalization can be held efficiently through full replication. This index is the broadest of the well-known, widely distributed indexes that exclude illiquid, hard-to-trade stocks. Narrower U.S. equity

---

[5]Because they include a large number of micro-cap stocks, the broadest indexes also suffer from "stale" prices. Stocks that don't trade every day—typically the smallest-cap stocks—are carried at their most recent trade prices, which may not be very recent, or are priced at a broker's bid price or at the average of bid and ask. Other illiquid asset classes for which stale pricing is a problem in index construction are real estate, private equity, some types of corporate and municipal bonds, and the equity markets of some (typically emerging) countries. Stale prices cause the return and risk of a benchmark or portfolio to be misstated. Stale pricing has only a small impact, however, on broad-cap indexes.

[6]ETFs are investment funds (typically index funds), shares of which are traded on an exchange like any other stock. Thus, the investor pays and receives the market price, rather than the net asset value (NAV), for a share of an ETF. This characteristic is in contrast to conventional mutual fund shares, which are sold and redeemed by the fund management firm at the NAV. The market price of an ETF tends to remain close to the NAV because of the trading activity of brokers' arbitrage desks and because of the trades executed by the fund management firm itself.

indexes that are still considered broad-cap, such as the Dow Jones U.S. Total Market Index and the S&P 1500 Index, are also investable.

The Russell 1000 and S&P 500, which are large-cap indexes, are eminently investable as long as you don't try to buy a stock that has limited float and that has just been selected for the S&P 500 (see the discussion of free-float mismatch in Chapter 7).

Reconstitution Frequency vs. Turnover. Reconstitution—the process of periodically deciding which stocks meet the criteria for inclusion in the index—is a source of turnover (which is costly to investors) because the manager must trade to keep pace with changes in index contents. Because timely reconstitution is what enables an index to accurately track the asset class it is designed to represent, there is a trade-off between such accuracy and trading costs.

Turnover resulting from tracking reconstitution is a major concern for managers of small-cap and style indexes, where companies with a large weight in the index are constantly crossing the size or style boundaries that qualify them for inclusion. For this reason, the constructors of size and style indexes tend to reconstitute them at regular and rather infrequent intervals, such as quarterly or annually.

The lists of holdings of broad-cap indexes are much more stable. Broad-cap indexes tend to experience turnover in their smallest-cap stocks, making turnover less of a problem when measured by the weight in the index of the stocks being traded. So, continuous reconstitution (as is done with the Wilshire 5000 and S&P 500), although not necessarily ideal, is not a terrible burden on investors or managers. Nonetheless, turnover is costly whatever its source or volume, and a cost advantage accrues to indexes that have less of it.

In terms of reconstitution-related turnover and trading costs, indexes that have no fixed limit on the number of stocks and that are all-inclusive in terms of their capitalization range have a small but nontrivial advantage over indexes with a fixed number of stocks. The reason is that an all-inclusive index gains or loses stocks only because of new listings, delistings, and other changes in the identity of the stocks in the market. The holdings list of a fixed-count index, in contrast, typically changes also to reflect the shifts in the capitalization rankings of stocks that occur as their prices fluctuate. Of broad-cap U.S. equity indexes, the only all-inclusive one is the Wilshire 5000; those indexes with a fixed number of stocks include the Russell 3000 and S&P 500. These latter indexes tend to experience higher turnover and, consequently, higher transaction costs. The Dow Jones Total Market is nearly all-inclusive and behaves more like an all-inclusive index than a fixed-count one.

Rebalancing Frequency vs. Turnover. Rebalancing, which is different from reconstitution, is the process of adjusting the weights of stocks in the index for changes in the number of shares outstanding. Taking account of changes in the number of shares outstanding maintains the macro consistency and mean–variance efficiency of the index. A theoretically ideal index would continuously update the number of shares that a company has issued, but a trade-off is involved: The index fund manager must rebalance to reflect these changes, thereby imposing transaction costs on the investor. Thus, index constructors typically decide on a prearranged schedule for updating shares-outstanding data so that changes in the index will be somewhat predictable and index fund managers can decide how to rebalance. Active managers benchmarked to the index also find it useful to be able to predict changes in index contents.

Objective and Transparent Rules vs. Judgment. Some benchmarks are constructed on the basis of rules that are reasonably objective; others are constructed through the use of judgment. The advantage of objective rules is that any investor with access to the rules and the relevant data can predict fairly accurately what stocks will be added to and deleted from the index. This information enables investors to trade in anticipation of (rather than in reaction to) additions and deletions and, in general, to manage the index replication process in an orderly and efficient manner. Active managers also find such information useful.

The use of judgment in selecting stocks or other securities for an index allows the index constructor to achieve certain traits, however, that cannot be achieved through objective rules and that constructors of judgment-based indexes claim are desirable. Standard & Poor's, which uses judgment in selecting stocks for its S&P 500 and other indexes, asserts that its indexes are superior in terms of stability, accurate representation of the industry distribution of the economy, and other attributes. The S&P indexes can achieve these traits specifically because the index construction staff need not act mechanically in selecting and removing stocks and can take conscious steps to construct an index with the desired characteristics.[7]

Thus, the trade-off is between the clarity and predictability of a rule-based index and the flexibility of a judgment-based index.

---

[7]The use of judgment to select the S&P 500 has led to the allegation that the S&P 500 is itself an actively managed portfolio and thus should not be used as a benchmark for other active portfolios; Chapter 6 contains an assessment of this critique.

2. Using Benchmarks to Measure Performance

Just about everyone knows that the purpose of active management is to add alpha—extra return relative to a benchmark representing the asset class in which the manager is invested. How should you measure alpha? How should you measure active risk, the risk taken by the active manager in the hope of achieving that alpha? Most importantly, having decided how to measure alpha and active risk, what should you do with the information?

Regression Alpha and Subtraction Alpha

First, recall how the Greek letter α comes into the discussion. It is from the "market model" regression equation of Jensen (1968). The market model is

$$r_i = r_f + \alpha_i + \beta_i (r_m - r_f) + \tilde{\varepsilon}, \tag{2.1}$$

where

r_i = return on security or portfolio i

r_f = riskless rate of return

α_i = unexpected component of return—that is, unexpected if your expectations are formed by the capital asset pricing model (see Chapter 4); this alpha may also be regarded as the value added by the manager after adjustment for beta risk

β_i = amount of market risk represented by portfolio i, scaled so that the benchmark or market portfolio has a beta equal to 1.0

r_m = return on the cap-weighted market index

$\tilde{\varepsilon}$ = a random error term distributed around zero

In essence, the market model tells you to run a regression with alpha as one of the regression coefficients (results). Specifically, the alpha from Equation 2.1 is the manager's excess return, or value added, after adjusting for the amount of market risk (beta risk) taken. As suggested later, you should adjust for other risks, such as style risks, but in principle, if you use Equation 2.1, you have calculated a risk-adjusted alpha.

Now, a widespread current practice is to calculate alpha as

$$\alpha_i = r_i - r_m. \tag{2.2}$$

What is wrong with this picture? It contains no adjustment for risk. Suppose, for example, that the portfolio has a higher beta than the benchmark and that the portfolio outperformed the benchmark in a rising market. Wouldn't the investor want to know how much of the extra return was added through market exposure (beta) and how much is "real" alpha, value added? The subtraction alpha that Equation 2.2 provides wrongly attributes the reward for extra beta risk to the manager.[1] The regression alpha from Equation 2.1 is the real alpha, the alpha that controls for beta risk.

Later, I will push even further to "purify" the alpha by adjusting portfolio performance for style exposures (betas) as well as market beta. For now, however, simply note that a regression is required to calculate real alphas.

Dimensions of Active Management

Why should you care about getting as "pure" a measure of manager alpha as possible? Waring and Siegel wrote:

> You can't influence or control the return of your asset allocation policy [the policy for your mix of asset classes and/or style exposures]. The market is going to do what the market is going to do. Other than making a risk level decision—to be more or less aggressive in your [asset allocation]—you're just a passenger. But if you have skill at security selection (or market timing or sector rotation, any active process), you have some *control* over returns, and this will add value, pure alpha, over and above the return of the policy. The search for such alpha is, arguably, the investor's highest calling. (2003, p. 37)

In addition, Waring and Siegel pointed out that *market exposures* are inherently rewarded. No one would invest in risky markets if the markets didn't offer, *ex ante*, a risk premium over riskless assets. In contrast, *active exposures* are not inherently rewarded. No one should expect active decisions to produce superior returns just because they are active. Active management is a zero-sum game: The returns (before costs) of all active managers in an asset class must sum to the asset-class return, whether the market for securities in that asset class is "efficient" or not.

Waring and Siegel demonstrated that market exposures and pure alpha are separate and separable; these conditions are part of the geometry of the regression used to calculate the alpha. By "separate," I mean that the market, not the manager, determines the market (and style) returns and the market has no influence on pure alpha whatsoever. Similarly, the manager, not the market, determines the pure alpha through his or her skill, or lack of it, and

---

[1] Managers who vary their betas during the measurement period will have an alpha, either positive or negative, but one that should be attributed to tactical asset allocation (market timing) rather than to the security selection for which most managers are hired.

the manager has no influence on the market or style returns whatsoever. By clearly separating the manager's contribution from other factors in this way, you can make well-informed decisions about manager selection and structure—which is why investors seek to measure pure alpha.[2]

Next, Waring and Siegel suggested introducing adjustments for style risk and the measurement of pure active risk. The real dimensions of active management are pure alpha, pure active risk, and costs (which have been ignored up to now)—not the conventional dimensions of style boxes, historical performance horse races, and manager salesmanship. Moreover, as I show in Chapter 3, estimates of pure alpha and of pure active risk can be used to frame a "manager structure optimization" problem (to use the words of Waring, Pirone, Whitney, and Castille 2000) that is incremental to and independent of the more familiar asset-class optimization problem.

Multiple Regression: Adjusting for Style Risk

As researchers since the late 1970s have found, and as I discuss at length in Chapter 8, certain factors (usually called "styles") other than the broad market or beta factor help explain the return differences between one stock and another or between one portfolio and another. The most widely recognized style divisions are large company size (capitalization) versus small company size and value stock versus growth stock.[3]

Returns can be adjusted for exposure to style factors in a number of ways. One approach, developed by Fama and French (1993), uses "natural" or unconstrained regression to estimate exposure to style factors. Their three-factor model, the first regression equation in Chapter 8, is an estimate of the pure alpha or value added by the manager. All other things being equal, natural regression is preferable to constrained regression, but the Fama–French method has the disadvantage that its style factors are amorphous; you cannot obtain index funds offering pure exposure to the factors.

Sharpe (1988, 1992) devised a method that is similar in spirit to the three-factor model but different mathematically. In using Sharpe's model, the analyst estimates the portfolio of *style index funds* having the "best fit" to the active portfolio being analyzed. The style index funds usually used for this kind of analysis are large-cap value, large-cap growth, small-cap value, and small-cap growth (the "corner portfolios" in a style map). Cash must also be

---

[2]Following Waring, Pirone, Whitney, and Castille (2000), I use the term "manager structure" to mean the weights of the various managers in an overall investment program.

[3]In addition, some stocks and portfolios are classified as mid-cap (between large and small in capitalization) or "core" (between value and growth), but the estimation of pure alpha will not require these extra wrinkles.

included as a regressor so that the overall level of risk in the best-fit portfolio matches the risk of the portfolio being analyzed. The regression is usually constrained to have a nonnegative (that is, positive or zero) weight for each of the style index funds, and the portfolio may be long or short in cash.[4] An analyst may wish to include other factors—for example, the return on a bond index fund. The alpha from this regression is an estimate of the pure alpha or value added by the manager beyond what could be achieved with a mix of style index funds.

Pure active risk (sometimes denoted by ω, omega) is simply the standard deviation of the pure alpha term. The active manager's information ratio, IR, is given by

$$IR = \frac{\alpha}{\omega} \tag{2.3}$$

and measures the amount of pure active return delivered per unit of active risk taken.

I would argue that the delivery of the information ratio is the only thing active managers should try to achieve: They should seek to maximize their pure alpha per unit of active risk. And the delivery of the information ratio is the only thing for which active managers should be paid an active fee; market and style exposures can be obtained almost for free by the investor using index funds, exchange-traded funds, or derivatives.

Importance of Measuring Pure Alpha and Active Risk

Why is it necessary to measure pure alpha and pure active risk so carefully? For the investor looking backward at history to evaluate a manager's performance, Waring and Siegel wrote:

> [T]hese measures . . . properly separate investment results that are the investor's responsibility from those that are created by the manager. The returns delivered by the capital markets on the particular mix of styles that constitute the manager's custom benchmark are the responsibility of the investor who selected the manager, if only because the investor is the only party in a position to control the market risk exposures across his or her whole portfolio of managers.
>
> Too often, performance evaluation practices confuse the benchmark return and the pure alpha, apportioning credit and blame incorrectly. Even the smartest and most well intentioned investors are sorely tempted to blame the active manager, rather than themselves, when the manager's asset class delivers a poor policy return (no matter what pure alpha the manager achieved). With the pure active return and risk clearly defined and calculated, these errors need no longer occur. (pp. 38–39)

---

[4] If the regression is unconstrained, allowing leveraged or short "positions" in one or more style benchmarks, the "fit" of the regression is better—that is, the regression provides a better model of the manager.

The future cannot be forecasted with anything like the precision achieved in measuring the past. But as I point out in Chapter 3, you need forecasts of manager alphas for building portfolios of managers (the level of selection at which most investors operate) in the portfolio construction or optimization problem, just as you need forecasts of stock-by-stock alphas in building portfolios of stocks. Specifically, the problem of constructing a portfolio of managers requires that you develop forecasts of pure active risk and pure active return for the various managers that you are dealing with already or considering.

In the next chapter, I turn to framing manager selection as an optimization problem that uses the pure active return and risk defined here as the inputs. I also describe how a portfolio of managers that reflects these principles might look. Once these concepts and methods have been presented, I can return to the discussion of benchmarks.

3. Building Portfolios of Managers

Policy (market and style) risk and active risk are separate and separable. In other words, investors should decide first what policy risks to take and how much of each, and only after that task has been completed should the investor decide how to implement these allocations by selecting a *portfolio of managers*. In this chapter, manager selection is framed as an optimization problem that uses the pure active return and risk defined in Chapter 2 as the inputs and I describe what such a portfolio of managers might look like. To set the stage, I begin with expected utility and mean–variance optimization.

Expected Utility

One of the first principles of investing is that the investor should seek to maximize expected utility, which is equal to the expected return minus a penalty for risk:

$$E(U_i) = E(r_i) - \lambda_j E(\sigma_i^2), \tag{3.1}$$

where

$E(U_i)$ = expected incremental utility of portfolio i in the investor's overall portfolio

$E(r_i)$ = expected return of portfolio i

λ_j = risk-aversion parameter for investor j (that is, the rate at which investor j translates risk into a negative return, or disutility; note that this parameter differs from one investor to another)

$E(\sigma_i^2)$ = the expected variance of portfolio i

Now, with so many asset choices, how do you figure out whether each choice provides *incremental* utility—that is, whether the combination of assets selected adds enough expected return to justify the extra risk? In other words, how do you *maximize* expected utility? The answer is through Markowitz mean–variance optimization (MVO). Managers can be considered to be asset choices like any other. Waring and Siegel wrote:

> Building a portfolio of managers is like building a portfolio of anything—it's all about balancing risk and return, trying to find the best trade-off. Optimization is the technology that explicitly calculates these trade-offs in search of the highest-utility portfolio (of anything) for a given investor. (2003, p. 39)

To make optimization useful in a manager-selection framework, you must first invoke the separation principle between policy risk and active risk. The trade-offs involved in asset allocation (that is, in determining the policy mix) are resolved by MVO through use of the utility function in Equation 3.1 with risk-aversion parameter λ specific to the investor; the result is the optimal mix of asset-class exposures for that investor. Next, you can perform a parallel calculation—also involving an optimizer, albeit a special-purpose one—for the managers. In this optimization, you use the expected pure alpha and expected active risk estimates as discussed in Chapter 2. You also use a utility function for active risk similar in form to Equation 3.1 but expressing the investor's aversion, not to total risk but to the active risk added by a manager. Waring and Siegel noted that for most investors, the active-risk-aversion parameter is several times larger than the policy-risk-aversion parameter.[1] This second step, optimization across manager alphas, is incremental to the first step and preserves the asset mix decided on in the first step. Waring, Pirone, Whitney, and Castille (2000), who provided the full details needed to implement the method, refer to this second step as manager structure optimization (or MSO, in homage to Markowitz's MVO).

Critiques of Optimization

Some investors are reluctant to put optimization into practice because they regard optimizers as error maximizers that cause inaccurate inputs to be translated into potentially even more inaccurate portfolio weights. This criticism has been enunciated by Richard Michaud in several well-known works (see Michaud 1998, 2003; Michaud and Michaud 2003).

The Michaud critique is technically correct: Optimizer inputs, because they are statistical estimates, are necessarily inexact. There is no way to make the precise estimates that would be needed for absolute confidence in the outputs of an optimizer. Mark Kritzman has persuasively argued, however:

> We would be naive if we expected optimization to convert valueless return and risk estimates into efficient portfolios. Rather, we optimize to *preserve* whatever value there is in our . . . estimates when we translate them into portfolios. . . . Optimization is a process that determines the most favorable tradeoff between competing interests. In portfolio management, the competing interests are return enhancement and risk reduction. . . . If we don't optimize, we will fail to translate even valuable inputs into efficient portfolios. Therefore, both good inputs and optimization are necessary . . . but neither by itself is sufficient. (2003, p. 1; italics modified from the original)

---

[1]Therefore, most investors would rather take policy risk than active risk. This choice makes sense because policy risk is inherently rewarded, on average, over time whereas active risk is not (because active management is a zero-sum game).

Now, where are these good inputs going to come from when you are building portfolios of managers?

Forecasting Manager Alphas

As Waring and Siegel pointed out, investors make implied forecasts of all their managers' alphas (plus active risk and other parameters) simply by holding whatever manager mix they happen to have. These implied forecasts can be backed out through "reverse optimization." Many investors would be surprised at how large their implied expected alphas for managers are.

Rather than heuristically deciding (say, through a system of filling style boxes) what your manager mix ought to be, you could, instead, explicitly use a special-purpose optimizer to select the manager weights. The required inputs are

- the expected pure alpha and pure active risk for each manager,
- the mix of market and style factors to which each manager is exposed, and
- the return–risk correlation matrix of the factors themselves.[2]

Of these inputs, the tricky one is, of course, the forecast of manager alphas. The discipline required to forecast manager alphas is similar to that required to forecast security alphas for use in a security-level optimizer. The most important caveat is to avoid simply extrapolating past performance into the future; winning managers (or stocks) don't persist with any degree of certainty. You must take into account fundamental and qualitative factors as well as quantitative factors. In the end, you will probably not be fully confident of the forecasts—which is just as it should be. No one makes perfect forecasts. Moreover, manager alpha forecasts don't have to be extraordinarily good to add value (when used in an optimization context); they only have to be more right than wrong.

But without an alpha forecast that represents at least the midpoint estimate of the investor's expectation for the manager, what justification does the investor have for using that manager instead of a mix of index funds representing the same market and style exposures? Alpha forecasts are necessary, if only as a conceptual exercise, to make sure you aren't being unduly swayed by past performance and manager salesmanship. And, having made these alpha forecasts, the investor can take them beyond the conceptual level and actually use them in a manager-level optimizer to build the portfolio. The issue is one of responsibility and accountability: If an investor is going to build a

---

[2]You also need the correlation matrix of the active returns of the managers, but this matrix can usually be presumed to be a matrix of zeros (because regression on the market and style factors causes the residuals to be mostly uncorrelated, at least for large-cap U.S. equity managers).

portfolio that includes active managers, that investor should be able to defend the alpha forecasts that are, implicitly or explicitly, embedded in the portfolio's composition. Otherwise, the investor should index.[3]

An Optimized Portfolio of Managers

My earlier discussion of expected utility in the context of manager selection can be summarized as follows: You must expect a manager's alpha to do more than simply be positive. It must be large enough to overcome the loss of utility from the active risk added by the manager. This observation has implications for the issues of whether to use active managers, what kinds of active managers to use, and what their weights should be.

Drawing on expected utility theory, Grinold (1990) and Kahn (2000) demonstrated that the holdings weight of manager i in the investor's total portfolio, h_i, is given by

$$h_i \sim E\left(IR_i \frac{1}{\omega_i}\right), \qquad (3.2)$$

where (given that E is the expectational operator) IR_i is the expected information ratio of manager i and ω_i is the expected active risk of manager i—that is, the expected volatility of the manager's pure alpha around a properly established benchmark. In other words, the manager's weight in the portfolio should be proportional to the manager's expected information ratio divided by the manager's active risk or, equivalently (recalling the definition of IR in Equation 2.1), the manager's expected alpha divided by the manager's active risk *squared*.

Thus, if you are going to take active risk, you should seek managers who not only have real skill (a high information ratio) but also exhibit low active risk—for example, enhanced index funds. Traditional medium-risk, long-only active managers would play a lesser role in the portfolio, and concentrated, high-risk, long-only active managers would have the least favored place. The Grinold and Kahn argument also gives a large weight to market-neutral (long–short) equity hedge funds for investors who are allowed to hold such positions.[4]

---

[3]Waring and Siegel expressed this concept as follows: "[A]n investor must meet *two conditions* if he or she is to hire active managers. First, one must believe that superior managers really do exist. That's easy, if one accepts that managers differ in their skill levels. Second—this is the hard one—one must believe that he or she can identify which ones will be the winners" (p. 46).

[4]Note that the general principle of keeping costs under control is violated with most market-neutral equity hedge funds. I hope that the extraordinarily high fees currently associated with hedge funds will be subject to competitive downward pressure, but pending that development, investors may have to pay such fees to obtain the benefits of this type of fund.

In summary, constructing a portfolio of managers is like any other portfolio construction problem: It calls for maximizing return while controlling risk, so it is an optimization problem. To solve such a problem, you need forecasts of manager alphas. Making such forecasts is analogous to active equity managers making forecasts for the stocks in their opportunity sets. It is the toughest job in finance, but if you are unable or unwilling to try to make such forecasts, you should simply index.

4. The Evolution of MPT and the Benchmarking Paradigm

Before the emergence of modern portfolio theory, the original paradigm for investment management called for portfolio managers to evaluate each investment on its merits and downplayed diversification. This approach gave way to mean–variance optimization and the capital asset pricing model, sometimes grouped together as modern portfolio theory or simply portfolio theory. MPT has, in turn, spawned a "benchmarking" paradigm, one in which benchmarks are used as the starting point for active portfolios and risk is defined as the degree of deviation from the benchmark. In this chapter, I trace that evolutionary path.

Portfolio Theory as a Scientific Paradigm

In 1962, Thomas Kuhn, the historian of science, characterized scientific revolutions as shifts in *paradigms* (established patterns of thinking) motivated by an accumulation of empirical evidence that the existing theories are not adequate to explain and predict observed phenomena (see Kuhn 1996). According to Kuhn, a crisis point is reached when anomalies (empirical observations that don't fit existing theory) become so troublesome that the need for a new theory is evident, at least to many researchers. The crisis is resolved when a new theory emerges, from the many being tested, that fits observed phenomena, thus eliminating the anomalies. Typically, although not always, the replacement of a strongly established theory by a new one meets with a great deal of resistance from adherents of the old theory. The iconic example is the replacement of the Ptolemaic (geocentric) theory of the solar system by the Copernican (heliocentric) theory in the 16th century.

First published in 1962, Kuhn's book—which, for all practical purposes, gave the word "paradigm" its current place in the English language—is one of the most influential books about science ever written. And it provides a basis for this exploration of benchmarks and benchmarking.

In the original investment paradigm, an investor had to justify each investment on its own merits. This view was largely replaced between about 1964 and 1980 by the body of knowledge loosely known as modern portfolio theory, which relies on capitalization-weighted benchmarks both as the starting point for building actively managed portfolios and as the reference asset for measuring the performance and risk of these portfolios.

A sort of crisis in MPT seemed to arise toward the end of the 1990s bull market, when cap-weighted benchmarks became highly risky because they included securities, at their market weights, that had swollen to huge caps despite having little intrinsic value. This apparent crisis brought to the surface concerns about MPT that had been submerged for a long time. Although no specific theory arose to replace MPT and although (as I argue later) MPT is mostly correct, some recent trends demonstrate that MPT is not fully predictive of investor behavior. The trends include, most notably, the popularity of hedge funds and an emphasis on achieving "absolute returns." Thus, the future of investing may incorporate non-MPT as well as MPT currents of thought.

The Original Paradigm

In the original pre-MPT paradigm, each investment in a portfolio is evaluated separately. The emphasis is on each investment's value, on finding investments that are intrinsically worth more than their current market prices.[1] Not much attention is paid to risk. Portfolio construction disciplines that seek not only to control risk but also to take advantage of the correlation structure of securities are not part of the original paradigm. Other than cash, investors have no "starting point" or "normal" portfolio to which they would retreat if they had no views on any security. The result of this way of thinking about investments is concentrated, and more or less equally weighted, portfolios.

As you will see in detail in a moment, performance measurement is also undeveloped in the original paradigm. Although benchmarks, including some very good ones (e.g., the S&P 90 Index, which is the forerunner of today's S&P 500 Index), existed in the time period when the original paradigm was dominant, the practice of comparing the performance of a particular portfolio with that of a benchmark wasn't widespread. Furthermore, no one knew how to risk-adjust the returns of a portfolio or benchmark so that fair comparisons could be made. That technology required the innovations of MPT.

John Burr Williams' classic 1938 textbook, *The Theory of Investment Value* (see Williams 1956), which introduced the dividend discount model (DDM), is an excellent example of original-paradigm thinking: Williams told investors how to find the *single best* stock and did not recommend (or even really mention) diversification.[2] John Maynard Keynes also thought diversification—

---

[1]Despite the emphasis on value, the growth style in investing is consistent with "original paradigm" thinking, as demonstrated in the excellent writings of Fisher (1958; reprinted 1996). A growth stock is a good value if the present value of its expected future cash flows (dividends plus liquidation price) is greater than its current price.

[2]Interestingly, Williams' discovery of the DDM predates by quite a few years the better-known (at least among academics) work of Gordon and Shapiro (1956).

"having a small gamble in a large number of different [companies]"—was a "travesty of investment policy" (quoted in Bernstein 1992, p. 48).

Other works of the pre-MPT period do, however, address the idea that investors don't have perfect foresight and thus face risk that can be mitigated by diversification. For example, in his 1949 book *The Intelligent Investor*, Benjamin Graham advised, "Diversification is an established tenet of conservative investment. . . . Even with a margin [of value over price] in the investor's favor, an individual security may work out badly" (see Graham and Zweig 2003, p. 518).

Thus, the investment paradigm that I have termed "original" embodied some common sense as well as some nonsense. It didn't quantify risk or even return (performance), and it paid only passing attention to diversification, but it set the stage for an orderly comparison of security prices with their fundamental values, a discipline still central to the practice of active portfolio management. As noted in Chapter 6, some of the tenets of the original paradigm are making a comeback as investors question the wisdom of MPT's prescriptions for investor behavior.

The Bad Old Days of No Performance Measurement

Before the capital asset pricing model (CAPM) provided a basis for the quantification of performance relative to a benchmark, investment returns could nevertheless be measured accurately. Fisher (1966), drawing directly on an algorithm created in the 17th century by Sir Isaac Newton and Joseph Raphson, provided a generalized method for calculating internal rates of return, of which the time-weighted rate-of-return calculation now used to measure investment performance is a simple extension.[3] And Cowles (1938) correctly recognized that total return, not price appreciation, is the proper metric of performance.

A retrospective by Jason Zweig, the illustrious financial historian and columnist for *Time* and *Money* magazines, shows, however, that performance measurement—to say nothing of benchmarking and quantitative performance evaluation—was pretty primitive until not long ago. As an example, Zweig

---

[3]According to Fisher (1966), the time-weighted rate of return is the linked internal rate of return, where a portfolio is valued at discrete time intervals and the internal rate of return (IRR) is calculated over the period between two successive valuation times; then, these IRRs are linked (by multiplying together terms consisting of 1 plus the IRR) to produce the time-weighted rate of return. See Fisher (1966), Newton (1664–1671), and Raphson (1690). I thank Ronald J. Surz for pointing out the connection between Fisher's work and the work, more than two and a half centuries earlier, of Newton and Raphson.

noted that even Graham, reflecting on the portfolio managed by his Graham-Newman Corporation in 1936–1956, glided over the problem:

> [Our] portfolio was always well diversified, with more than a hundred different issues represented. In this way [we] did quite well through many years of ups and downs in the general market; [we] averaged about 20 percent per annum on the several millions of capital [that we] had accepted for management, and [our] clients were well pleased with the results. (Graham and Zweig 2003, p. 532)

The clients should have been pleased: From the beginning of 1936 to the end of 1956, the S&P 90, one of the predecessors of the S&P 500, had a total return of only 12.2 percent a year. The casual style in which the information is presented, however, leads me to question whether the return was measured accurately—that is, after taking into account cash flows in and out of the fund, fees, and other factors. The recollection also makes no mention of risk. Zweig has also recalled:

> I believe it was not until the 1980s that mutual funds were required by the SEC [U.S. Securities and Exchange Commission] to calculate and report a number called "total return." When the SEC proposed that new rule (in the wake of the scandals over GNMA [Government National Mortgage Association] and other "government-plus" bond funds that cannibalized capital in pursuit of current yield), the fund industry met it with howls of execration. The most common refrain was that the investing public would not understand or would misinterpret a single total return figure. Previously, investors had either to calculate the number themselves or rely on services like Wiesenberger, Lipper, or the financial press. The oldest prospectus in my collection, the 1941 prospectus for Investment Company of America, provides a statement of profit and loss, a statement of earned surplus, and a statement of capital surplus, all for three fiscal years, along with a "computation of net asset value," along with a table of all dividends paid over the previous seven or eight years. But total return is not calculated, and performance is not measured against anything of any kind.
>
> By 1970, judging by my Mates Investment Fund prospectus, disclosure had not improved. "Capital changes" had four sub-captions: Net asset value at beginning of period, net realized and unrealized gains (losses), distribution from realized capital gains, net asset value at end of period. Total return is still not calculated, and no benchmark information is provided.[4]

Although precursors to any scientific discovery can usually be found without looking very hard, they are not apparent in the present case. Maybe nothing was happening. Bernstein may have summed up the zeitgeist of the period best by noting:

> Performance measurement was carried out . . . at cocktail parties, dinner parties, bridge games, and the golf course. At these locations, individuals boasted and moaned to one another about what their investment advisors were doing. This lively channel of communication was continuous rather than quarterly, and ignored adjustments for risk, which only made matters worse. Managers who could keep their heads when everyone around them was losing theirs were rare birds indeed. (1994, p. 1)

---

[4]Personal communication with Jason Zweig.

The Benchmarking Paradigm

Performance measurement, index funds, and "benchmarking" of active funds were made possible by MPT, which emerged in the 1950s and 1960s. The efforts of consultants, index providers, and seekers of "anomalies" or systematic rules to beat the market further enriched this fertile environment.[5]

The Markowitz Revolution. The young Harry Markowitz's University of Chicago Ph.D. dissertation (1952) set the original investment paradigm on its ear. "I was struck with the notion that you should be interested in risk as well as return," he wrote.[6] That a manager or analyst should be "interested" in risk doesn't sound all that revolutionary until you explore the consequences, preferably with mathematical tools.

Markowitz defined the risk of an investment as the period-to-period standard deviation of the investment's return.[7] If you accept that definition, Markowitz's observation leads you to try to build portfolios that maximize the expected return *at each given level of expected standard deviation*. Such portfolios are built by taking advantage of the correlation structure of the available securities—buying more than you otherwise would of a security that has a low (preferably, negative) correlation with the other securities in your portfolio. This complex calculation is best done by use of mean–variance optimization (MVO), an application of quadratic programming developed by Markowitz himself. The resulting portfolio is said to be "efficient," in that no portfolio can be constructed with a higher expected return at the same level of risk (or with the same expected return but a lower level of risk).

What does MVO have to do with benchmarks? Well, if a given portfolio is "optimal" (the most efficient portfolio that can be constructed), then it is a benchmark (in the English language sense) for those who would build portfolios. But because each investor has his or her own unique estimates for the expected returns and standard deviations of securities and for the correlations between them, the "most efficient" portfolio is different for each investor. No objective benchmark emerges from this analysis. Not until the contribution of Sharpe, more than a decade after Markowitz, does one appear.

---

[5]I thank Paul D. Kaplan of Morningstar for his helpful comments on this section.

[6]Markowitz noted that investors already behave as though they face risk; they diversify in practice rather than concentrating their holdings on the security perceived to be the best.

[7]This definition is itself a source of much controversy. I briefly compare standard deviation with other risk measures in Chapter 5.

Sharpe and the CAPM. In pursuit of a general theory of how assets are priced, Sharpe (among several others) noted that if all investors have the *same* expectations of return, risk, and correlation for every security, and if all investors hold efficient portfolios based on these expectations as described by Markowitz, the capitalization-weighted market portfolio itself is mean–variance efficient.[8] The CAPM requires other assumptions—most of them just as unlikely as the supposition that all investors see the same return–risk–correlation picture and use an optimizer—but for elegance, simplicity, and ease of use, the CAPM is difficult to beat, so it has won acceptance despite its reliance on stringent conditions.

If the cap-weighted market portfolio is mean–variance efficient, it is the best portfolio that you can build in the absence of special insight or skill. It should be the benchmark. This principle is strictly true only for portfolios with the same risk as the market, however, because expected return is related to risk. For portfolios with risk levels different from that of the market, an adjustment is necessary.

The CAPM posits that expected return is proportional to that component of risk (called beta) that represents correlation with the market. (By "the market," I mean the cap-weighted market index.) This relationship provides a framework for measuring the performance of portfolios with different risk levels: A portfolio manager adds value (called alpha) if he or she produces, after adjustment for the beta of the portfolio, a return that is greater than the market's return.[9] **Table 4.1** presents CAPM performance statistics for a sample of four managers—an index fund, a risk-controlled active (or "enhanced index") fund (BGI Alpha Tilts), a conventional active manager (Fidelity), and a hedge fund (First Eagle). The active managers in the example in Table 4.1 are all successful in the sense of adding alpha; in reality, most managers are not successful.[10]

Thus, the familiar concepts of quantitative performance measurement—with its alphas, betas, tracking errors, and R^2s—are made possible by the

---

[8]See Sharpe (1964). John Lintner, Jan Mossin, and Jack Treynor discovered the CAPM at about the same time as Sharpe. The story of the derivation of the CAPM is told compellingly in Bernstein (1992).

[9]A good general discussion of alpha, beta, and other statistics relevant to performance measurement is in Chapter 7 of Sharpe, Alexander, and Bailey (1995); for a strong discussion of the CAPM, see Chapter 10 of their work.

[10]In Chapter 2, I discussed adjusting portfolio performance for common factors—including style factors—in addition to the market, or beta, when measuring investment performance.

Table 4.1. Sample CAPM and Related Statistics for Selected Funds for the 60 Months Ending 31 March 2000

Fund	Compound Annual Total Return	Standard Deviation	Sharpe Ratio	CAPM Alpha	Alpha *t*-statistic	Information Ratio	CAPM Beta	Adjusted R^2
Vanguard 500 Index	26.70%	14.83%	1.348	–6 bps	–1.44	–0.661	1.001	1.000
BGI Alpha Tilts	27.82	15.06	1.389	70	0.82	0.598	1.009	0.986
Fidelity	26.99	14.45	1.396	191	0.76	0.044	0.912	0.871
First Eagle	27.58	14.36	1.437	488	1.20	0.091	0.786	0.652

Notes: The Sharpe ratio is calculated in excess of the U.S. Treasury bill return. The CAPM alpha and beta, alpha *t*-statistic, information ratio, and adjusted R^2 are relative to the S&P 500. The negative alpha, alpha *t*-statistic, and information ratio for the Vanguard 500 Index Fund result from fees and other expenses.

CAPM.[11] Some might argue that I am making too much of the connection between portfolio theory and benchmarks; after all, performance measurers would seek an objective reference point (in addition to peer group comparisons) even if there were no theory suggesting that the cap-weighted market is *a priori* efficient. And a cap-weighted index, because it requires no rebalancing when security prices change, is a convenient reference point. Portfolio theory, however, provided a powerful impetus to benchmarking: Virtually all investors know they have the option to index at low cost, and they know from their exposure to the basic ideas of portfolio theory that indexing has many desirable properties. Moreover, investors know that if they are going to take active risk (and pay active fees), the decision to do so must be justified by superior performance, which must be measured scientifically.

Performance measurement, however, is not all there is to "benchmarking." Benchmarking is more than constructing market indexes or index funds, and it is more than comparing performance with a properly risk-adjusted (and style-adjusted) market index. The real impact of benchmarking is the pull that benchmarks exert on *active* management through the tools discussed in the next section.

Barr Rosenberg and Factor Models. Cognizant that the market index, or benchmark, is (at least theoretically) the mean–variance-efficient portfolio in the absence of special views on the value of specific securities, any manager might think to build an active portfolio by starting with the benchmark weights, then changing them according to his or her active views. But this is only a conceptual approach, not a scientific discipline. The role of benchmarks in scientifically managing active portfolios was firmly established by Barr Rosenberg, a University of California at Berkeley professor who developed a technique for quantitatively managing active risk (tracking error versus the

---

11 Formally, conventional performance measurement relies on the "market model," a backward-looking model with a functional form similar to that of the CAPM but somewhat different in purpose. Specifically, the CAPM seeks to estimate the expected return on an asset or portfolio; the market model seeks to apportion the actual past return between the part arising from market exposure (beta) and the part arising from active bets (alpha). But (and this aspect is rarely pointed out) the market model and the CAPM are not as different as this description makes them sound, because the market model gives accurate measures of the alpha added by the manager only if the CAPM is "true" (that is, if the CAPM gives accurate estimates of the return you should expect from the market or beta component). The method I set forth in Chapter 2, which measures performance after adjusting for size and valuation as well as beta, relies on a three-factor model of security returns (instead of the CAPM) being "true."

benchmark). To do so, he integrated two concepts (see Rosenberg 1974; Rosenberg and Marathe 1975):
1. You should optimize active return against active risk just as you optimize policy (market) return against policy risk.[12]
2. Returns on securities are characterized by "extra-market covariance"; that is, security returns are correlated with factors *other* than the market factor. (The market model says that security returns are correlated only with the market factor and are otherwise independent of one another.) As a result, you can model any security as a bundle of factor exposures plus an unexplained risk term. Such a model provides a better estimate of beta for use in the CAPM to determine expected security returns than can be obtained by calculating an ordinary historical regression beta for the security.

Here is the link between the two concepts: To solve the active return–active risk optimization problem at the individual-security level, you need forecasts of return and risk for every security in your opportunity set and you need forecasts of the correlation of every security with every other security. As a result, if the opportunity set is, say, the 3,000 stocks in the Russell 3000, you have $(3{,}000 \times 2{,}999)/2 = 4{,}498{,}500$ correlations to forecast (setting aside, for the moment, the risk and return forecasts). But if you have a model that characterizes each security as a bundle (or vector) of, say, 13 factors—the number of major factors in Rosenberg's best-known U.S. equity model, the Aegis model—then you have to forecast only the correlations of the *factors,* of which there are $(13 \times 12)/2 = 78$, plus the $(3{,}000 \times 13) = 39{,}000$ "loadings" (the degree of exposure of each security to each of the factors). Although 39,078 is still a daunting number, it is a manageable one, at least if you have the requisite software (which, helpfully, is sold by Barra—the company founded by Rosenberg—as well as by several competitors).[13] Most investment managers shortcut the problem further by drastically reducing the number of stocks under consideration.

In other words, the reason you need to build factor models of securities is to reduce the number of estimates needed to solve the active return–active risk optimization problem. Establishing this link and providing the technology to make the forecasts required by the factor model is Rosenberg's unique contribution, and it is this technology that led to the widespread practice of

---

[12]I used this insight in Chapter 3 in arguing that you should use active return–active risk optimization at the total portfolio level to select managers, but the concept originated with Rosenberg, who carried out this kind of optimization at the security level decades earlier.

[13]A good overview of the Barra model is at www.barra.com/research/barrapub/ risk_models.asp. Rosenberg is no longer personally associated with Barra.

benchmarking—in the sense of managing active portfolios by controlling their degree of departure from cap-weighted benchmarks.

With Barra's or similar tools, the investor can build quantitative active portfolios. The 13 major factors enumerated in Barra's Aegis model are shown in **Table 4.2**, together with sample factor "loadings" for some stocks and portfolios analyzed by using this factor approach. Factor loadings are expressed as Z-scores—that is, as the number of standard deviations by which a stock's or portfolio's exposure to a given factor differs from the average (or market) exposure to that factor. Table 4.2 indicates that General Motors has a dividend-yield factor exposure of 1.45, which means that General Motors' dividend yield (which is 6.5 percent) is almost one and a half standard deviations larger than the approximately 2 percent dividend yield of the cap-weighted market portfolio.

Table 4.2. Barra Risk-Factor Loadings for Two Mutual Funds and Two Stocks, 30 September 2002

	Mutual Funds		Stocks	
Risk Factor	Janus Twenty	Vanguard S&P 500 Index	Intel	General Motors
Market beta (S&P 500)	1.15	1.00	1.68	1.15
Market beta (ALLUS)	1.19	1.03	1.74	1.20
Volatility	0.09	–0.01	1.04	0.22
Momentum	0.08	–0.11	–0.58	–0.03
Size	1.04	0.38	1.07	0.01
Size nonlinearity	0.16	0.11	0.19	0.11
Trading activity	0.01	0.01	0.17	1.25
Growth	0.52	–0.05	–0.49	–0.56
Earnings yield	–0.12	0.03	–0.25	1.56
Value	0.22	–0.05	–0.08	1.71
Earnings variation	0.08	–0.06	–0.20	0.81
Leverage	–0.48	–0.10	–0.68	3.38
Currency sensitivity	0.52	0.00	–0.23	0.20
Dividend yield	–0.31	0.05	–0.53	1.45
Nonestimation universe	0.06	0.02	0.00	0.00

Notes: Factor loadings are relative to the Barra ALLUS (Barra All-U.S.) Index. The "nonestimation universe" factor is 0 if a company is in the Barra estimation universe and 1.0 if it is not. The nonestimation universe factor loading for mutual funds depends on the weight of stocks in the fund that are not in Barra's estimation universe.

Source: Barra.

The Role of Consultants. In the late 1970s and in the 1980s, as the technology for estimating active risk became accessible and as the importance of the new academic theories (the CAPM, efficient markets, and so forth) became widely appreciated, traditional active managers, in addition to "quants" and indexers, began to use this technology. This expansion of the role of quantitative investment analysis was led by the consultant community and resulted in the near universality of benchmarking seen today.

A.G. Becker Funds Evaluation Group was the consulting firm responsible for much of this innovation.[14] In the early 1970s, Becker had an absolute majority of pension fund assets under consulting advisement, according to a Greenwich Associates survey, but the firm's role was pretty much limited to calculating rates of return on its clients' portfolios as best it could in light of the data limitations. When John O'Brien (one of the founders of Wilshire Associates) joined Becker in the mid-1970s, however, he brought with him Gilbert Beebower, Richard Ennis, and David Booth (among other luminaries), who shared a passionate interest in MPT. The new Becker team introduced CAPM statistics and other practices of MPT to the vast consulting base that Becker already had, setting the stage for the widespread adoption of MPT and the benchmarking paradigm. Becker's base of consulting clients included many investment management firms as well as plan sponsors (pensions, foundations, and endowments), so not only the supply of investment management services but also the demand for services was affected by this new thinking.

Investment consulting organizations with the capabilities of calculating CAPM statistics, using optimizers to build portfolios, and otherwise implementing MPT ideas proliferated in the 1980s. Today, virtually all investment consulting firms have these capabilities, and small as well as large plan sponsors use these firms' services. Thus, the current large role of "benchmarked" portfolios may be regarded, in part, as an outgrowth of the increasing importance of investment consultants (and academics) in the interplay between investment management firms and their customers.

The Role of Index Providers. A final source of impetus toward the use of benchmarks, both to build index funds and as a starting point for active management, is the commercial index construction industry. When large profits are to be made by selling something, great effort is expended to increase the public's need or desire for it. Licensing fees are the source of profit in the index business. (An index provider, or constructor, collects licensing fees from managers who publicly announce that they are using the

---

14I thank Ronald J. Surz of Performance Presentation Consulting Alliance, who was at one time an executive of Becker, for providing the interview on which this section is based.

index as the basis for a fund or as a benchmark. Of course, various free-rider problems crop up.) Standard & Poor's pioneering role was documented in the Preface, and the emergence of index funds based on the S&P 500 and the rapidly spreading use of that index as a benchmark for active portfolios greatly increased that company's visibility in index provision, in contrast to its traditional role in providing debt ratings. Unfortunately for Standard & Poor's, it did not foresee the importance of index funds and did not position itself to receive large licensing fees.

A contrasting experience was that of the investment management firm Capital International, which introduced international equity benchmarks in 1969 (see Chapter 10) and built a successful business around index-associated fees. The consulting world made the next big push. In addition to Wilshire Associates, the Frank Russell Company played a crucial early role in bringing benchmarks to market. Finally, such brokerage firms as Salomon Brothers (now Citigroup) and Lehman Brothers, because they had the only real source of price information in the fixed-income market, became the natural providers of benchmarks in that market. And these firms retain their position as the principal sources of fixed-income benchmarks today.

Conclusion

Cap-weighted market indexes, which represent the theoretically mean–variance-efficient portfolio of securities in a given asset class, have been pressed into duty as performance *benchmarks*. An outgrowth of this transformation of meaning is the benchmarking paradigm, which comprises the following ideas:

- The market portfolio, proxied by a cap-weighted benchmark, is the portfolio with the lowest expected risk in a given asset class (among fully invested portfolios—that is, portfolios with a beta of 1.0 measured relative to the asset class).
- Policy risk and active risk are separate and separable; only when you have arrived at a policy decision (that is, when you have selected asset-class weights) should you implement that decision by selecting asset-class managers.
- Active management can be viewed as taking active bets against a benchmark. In other words, each security in the benchmark can be held at the benchmark weight (which represents no active risk) or at a greater or lesser weight (which represents some active risk). You can also take active risk by holding securities that aren't in the benchmark. Thus, any active portfolio can be understood as an index fund plus a portfolio of long and short positions relative to the benchmark.

- Following this logic, *not* to own the benchmark weight in a security is an active decision that, mathematically, must add to risk. Even if the particular security has little risk or is perceived as diversifying or removing the risk of other investments in the portfolio, you cannot actually subtract risk by deviating from the benchmark. You can, however, add alpha.
- Active management has only one legitimate role, which is to add expected utility by adding pure alpha minus a penalty for the active risk taken in the effort to add pure alpha (see Chapter 2). In less technical terms, active managers should try to add pure alpha while controlling the amount of active risk they take.

The idea that the benchmark is the portfolio with the lowest risk among fully invested portfolios in a given asset class is sometimes misunderstood as a claim that "index funds have no risk." No one seriously believes that index funds in risky asset classes have no risk. They have policy risk, which is most of the risk in any investment.

5. The 1990s Bubble and the Crisis in MPT

The 1980s and 1990s, which hosted the greatest bull market ever known, were friendly to the new academic and consulting climate that emphasized index funds, actively managed portfolios based on (or "benchmarked to") market-capitalization-weighted indexes, and quantitative control of active risk (or tracking error). With U.S. equity markets rising at an astonishing 20 percent annual rate, your chief risk was being out of the market—or taking active positions that would cause your return to depart from the market return.[1] The volume of assets indexed to, or actively managed but benchmarked to, cap-weighted indexes grew and grew.

Not that all investors and managers were happy with the state of affairs or that portfolios with high active risk did not sometimes earn outsize returns. An article by Clifford, Kroner, and Siegel (2001) revealed that the best-performing portfolio (as measured by the CAPM alpha) over the 20 years and 3 months from January 1980 through March 2000 was Berkshire Hathaway, which had an alpha of 8 percentage points a year and a tracking error against the S&P 500 Index of 22.6 percent.[2] The Driehaus Small Growth Fund, which also had a stellar alpha, had an even larger tracking error. There are a number of other such stories, but not many; in general, because most managers subtract, rather than add, alpha (at least after fees and other costs are considered), the path to riches in the bull market was to stay invested in the equity market and to avoid tracking error. The ready access to technology that enabled managers to measure and control tracking error (and the growing difficulty in adding alpha as markets became more efficient) reinforced this trend.

By the turn of the millennium, when the bull market had run for almost 18 years (with a couple of dramatic interruptions), culminating in a super-boom in technology and other growth issues between 1998 and early 2000, cap-weighted indexes had taken on an odd character. As shown in **Table 5.1**, only

---

[1]To be precise, the total return on the S&P 500 Index, including reinvestment of dividends, was 19.75 percent a year, compounded, from 1 September 1982 to 31 March 2000.

[2]Although Berkshire Hathaway is structured as an operating company and is traded on the New York Stock Exchange, it is best understood as a portfolio (that is, as an investment manager) and compared with other portfolios (mutual funds, separately managed accounts, and so forth).

Table 5.1. Financial Data for 30 Largest U.S. Stocks by Capitalization, 31 March 2000

Rank	Name	Price per Share	Market Cap (millions)	EPS	Dividends per Share	P/E	Dividend Yield
1	Microsoft	$106.25	$553,016	$1.62	$0	65.8	0%
2	Cisco Systems	77.31	537,796	0.73	0	106.5	0
3	General Electric	155.63	512,833	3.32	1.64	46.9	1.05
4	Intel	131.94	440,935	2.50	0.12	52.8	0.09
5	Exxon Mobil	77.94	271,214	2.95	1.76	26.4	2.26
6	Wal-Mart	56.50	251,636	1.33	0.24	42.5	0.42
7	Oracle	78.06	220,256	0.82	0	95.2	0
8	IBM	118.00	211,664	3.89	0.48	30.3	0.41
9	Citigroup	59.88	200,964	3.31	0.64	18.1	1.07
10	Lucent	61.25	195,233	0.85	0.08	72.1	0.13
11	AT&T	56.31	179,905	2.08	0.88	27.1	1.56
12	Nortel Networks	126.13	177,665	0.33	0.15	382.2	0.12
13	AIG	109.50	169,532	3.36	0.20	32.5	0.18
14	Sun Microsystems	93.69	163,669	1.61	0	58.3	0
15	AOL Time Warner	67.44	153,877	0.36	0	187.3	0
16	Home Depot	64.50	148,502	1.08	0.16	59.7	0.25
17	Merck	62.13	143,917	2.62	1.16	23.7	1.87
18	SBC Communications	42.13	143,199	2.26	0.98	18.6	2.33
19	Pfizer	36.56	140,729	0.92	0.36	39.9	0.98
20	Dell	53.94	138,358	0.73	0	73.9	0
21	EMC	126.00	134,161	1.25	0	100.8	0
22	Texas Instruments	160.00	130,663	2.09	0.17	76.6	0.11
23	Coca-Cola	46.94	116,051	1.31	0.68	35.8	1.45
24	Bristol Myers Squibb	58.00	114,631	1.94	0.98	29.9	1.69
25	Qualcomm	149.31	105,749	3.45	0	43.3	0
26	Motorola	146.00	104,337	2.33	0.48	62.6	0.33
27	Johnson & Johnson	70.25	97,643	3.07	1.12	22.9	1.59
28	Morgan Stanley	82.88	94,219	9.60	0.80	8.6	0.97
29	Yahoo!	171.38	90,226	0.61	0	280.9	0
30	BellSouth	46.88	88,211	2.11	0.76	22.2	1.62

Notes: Earnings, dividends, P/Es, and dividend yields are annualized. Earnings (as reported by Compustat) include "basic" earnings per share (EPS) adjusted to remove (1) the cumulative effect of accounting changes, (2) discontinued operations, (3) extraordinary items, and (4) special items.

Source: Ford Foundation, based on Compustat, Bridge, DAIS, and IDC data.

one of the top thirty U.S. stocks as ranked by capitalization on 31 March 2000 had a price-to-earnings ratio below 15 (roughly the average historical P/E of the market). Five of the top thirty stocks had a P/E higher than 100, and nine more had a P/E between 50 and 100. The market capitalization of the 14 largest companies in Table 5.1 with P/Es higher than 50 sums to $3.2 trillion. If these P/Es were ever to be "rationalized"—brought in line with reality—either the companies' earnings would have to grow at extraordinary rates for many years or the capitalization of the market would have to fall by some large fraction of $3.2 trillion.

You know what happened. By 30 September 2002, the capitalization of the 14 largest companies had fallen by $2.5 trillion as part of an overall equity market decline that trimmed more than $6 trillion from total U.S. equity capitalization. The proportion of the loss in capitalization that is represented by these few very large, and seemingly very overpriced, companies is remarkable.

After such a fiasco, the benchmarks, index funds, and benchmarked active portfolios became easy targets for critics. Who in their right mind would invest in such overpriced companies—even if, to avoid them, you had to take the "risk" of having large tracking error to a cap-weighted benchmark?

One (possibly too academic) answer is that many people had thought carefully about what the fair prices for technology and other popular growth companies should be and that the prices shown in Table 5.1 are the results of their analysis, as expressed through the supply of and demand for securities. Not many investors were absolutely sure at the time that the market was overpriced or that the cap-weighted benchmark was an *ex ante* inefficient portfolio. Many value managers and tactical asset allocators, to their credit, seemed sure, but they appear to have been a minority.[3]

On 31 March 2000 and for a period of time before and after, the cap-weighted benchmark was not a good portfolio to hold, *ex ante,* and an investor could have arrived at that conclusion through conventional analysis (cash flow or dividend discount models, relative-value or P/E analysis, and so forth). Many—even most—investment professionals could have added alpha simply by betting against the most obviously overvalued companies. But this bubble and its bursting were a once-in-a-generation anomaly. These events are not cause for a general indictment of modern portfolio theory (MPT) and of benchmarks. No sensible person ever said benchmarks were always and everywhere the best portfolios.

---

[3]Among the investment managers who publicly took this position were Robert D. Arnott of First Quadrant, Clifford S. Asness of AQR Capital Management, and Jeremy Grantham of Grantham, Mayo, Van Otterloo, & Company.

The top 30 U.S. equities by capitalization as of 30 September 2002 (that is, after the bear market) are shown in **Table 5.2**. With the excesses of the bubble era corrected—perhaps more than corrected—it is much less obvious how to avoid overpriced securities or otherwise build a portfolio that is more efficient than the cap-weighted benchmark. Of course, opportunities always exist for astute active managers, but the idea that cap-weighted indexes are fundamentally unsuited for service as portfolios (index funds) or as benchmarks for active management has lost much of its appeal.

Critiques of MPT and Conventional Finance

The bubble gave great encouragement, naturally, to anti-MPT factions, who had been raising sometimes valid critiques but rarely scoring a win in earlier years.[4] The most compelling critique came from behavioral finance, but other criticisms are also noteworthy.

Behavioral Finance. Efficient markets and MPT have been attacked from many angles. What distinguishes the behavioral finance school of thought from other critiques of MPT and benchmarks is that the behaviorists have the beginnings of a real theory and strong evidence for their positions.

Behavioral finance emanates from the observation by Rolf Banz, Sanjoy Basu, and many others (see Chapter 8) that the markets contain "anomalies"—Thomas Kuhn's word again—that is, patterns that are not consistent with efficient markets and other tenets of conventional finance and that are, consequently, a challenge to the conventional theories. At the same time that empirical researchers were documenting market anomalies—"small caps beat large caps" and "value beats growth" are the best known—other researchers, with more of a psychological bent, were examining the mistakes made by investors in framing and implementing investment decisions. This group of investigators—led by the Nobel Prize–winning researcher Daniel Kahneman, the late Amos Tversky, and the writing team of Hersh Shefrin and Meir Statman—produced the literature on behavioral finance that represents the most successful challenge yet to efficient markets and MPT. A full treatment of behavioral finance is in Shefrin (2002).

Among the mistakes made by investors are the following:

- overconfidence in one's own abilities,
- over- or underreaction to new information,

---

[4]MPT is sometimes used to describe a wide range of beliefs and practices, but I am defining MPT narrowly to comprise mean–variance optimization, the separation of policy and active risk, and the calculation and management of active risk as defined by the capital asset pricing model and factor models.

Table 5.2. Financial Data for 30 Largest U.S. Stocks by Capitalization, 30 September 2002

Rank	Name	Price per Share	Market Cap (millions)	EPS	Dividends per Share	P/E	Dividend Yield
1	General Electric	$24.65	$245,254	$1.59	$0.73	15.5	2.96%
2	Microsoft	43.74	234,598	1.10	0	39.8	0
3	Wal-Mart	49.24	217,771	1.73	0.28	28.5	0.57
4	Exxon Mobil	31.90	215,562	1.56	0.92	20.4	2.88
5	Pfizer	29.02	179,624	1.47	0.52	19.7	1.79
6	Johnson & Johnson	54.08	160,906	2.21	0.80	24.5	1.47
7	Citigroup	29.65	150,057	2.87	0.70	10.3	2.36
8	AIG	54.70	142,805	2.85	0.18	19.2	0.33
9	Coca-Cola	47.96	119,052	1.77	0.80	27.1	1.67
10	Procter & Gamble	89.38	116,238	3.62	1.52	24.7	1.70
11	Berkshire Hathaway A	73,900.00	113,349	2,729.00	0	27.1	0
12	Merck	45.71	102,828	3.15	1.42	14.5	3.11
13	IBM	58.31	98,796	4.16	0.59	14.0	1.01
14	Bank of America	63.80	95,868	5.65	2.44	11.3	3.82
15	Intel	13.89	92,577	0.58	0.08	23.9	0.58
16	Philip Morris	38.80	82,018	4.69	2.44	8.3	6.29
17	Wells Fargo	48.16	81,812	3.22	1.10	15.0	2.28
18	Cisco Systems	10.48	76,356	0.16	0	65.5	0
19	Verizon	27.44	74,868	3.38	1.54	8.1	5.61
20	Chevron Texaco	69.25	73,964	1.93	2.80	35.9	4.04
21	Viacom B	40.55	71,556	0.81	0	50.1	0
22	SBC Communications	20.10	66,834	2.33	1.07	8.6	5.30
23	PepsiCo	36.95	65,483	1.91	0.60	19.3	1.61
24	Abbott Laboratories	40.40	63,116	2.11	0.92	19.1	2.26
25	Eli Lilly	55.34	62,173	2.49	1.24	22.2	2.24
26	Home Depot	26.10	61,495	1.59	0.20	16.4	0.77
27	Dell	23.51	60,887	0.77	0	30.5	0
28	Fannie Mae	59.54	59,290	6.15	1.32	9.7	2.22
29	Amgen	41.70	53,300	1.34	0	31.1	0
30	UBS AG	41.00	53,099	2.75	0	14.9	0

Note: See notes to Table 5.1.

Source: Ford Foundation, based on Compustat, Bridge, DAIS, and IDC data.

- optimism (pessimists drop out of the game),
- pathological risk aversion (this trait is not inconsistent with optimism, because different investors make different mistakes at different times), and
- "frame dependence"—the difficulty that investors have in separating the verbal or mathematical form of a question, or the setting in which the question is asked, from the true economic content of the question.

In short, investors are not rational economic agents but human beings with limited cognitive ability and susceptibility to greed, fear, and foolishness who are forced to act in conditions of incomplete information. Welcome to the real world.

Behaviorists have been accused of shaping their theories to fit empirical facts, but they have rarely been charged with having a shortage of facts to support their cause. A great deal of empirical evidence supports the conclusion that the behaviorists are onto something. For example, "experimental economics" techniques (pioneered by Vernon Smith, who shared the 2002 Nobel Prize in Economics with Kahneman) have been used to demonstrate that in laboratory conditions (where, admittedly, the subjects of investigation may not have to live with the real-world consequences of their decisions), investors overreact to certain kinds of information and underreact to others, persistently overestimate their own abilities, and have difficulty avoiding frame dependence.

What behavioral finance implies is that markets cannot really be efficient. Their argument goes beyond acknowledging that some mispriced assets always exist. The bubble of 1998–2000 is evidence that the whole market can become mispriced; technology and Internet stocks were mispriced by large multiples for quite a while.[5] Thus, the bubble gave the behaviorists the push they needed to mount a challenge to conventional finance. And their view is widely accepted, at least in rough outline: Almost no one believes any more that markets are completely efficient.

If behavioral finance paints a true picture of the world, holding benchmarks as portfolios (that is, holding index funds) is not generally a good idea because it is engaging in "herd behavior." Holding the benchmark means holding a disproportionate weight in the most popular companies, which have the highest prices relative to their fundamental values.

What behavioral finance does *not* say is that cap-weighted benchmarks are irrelevant as a basis for measuring performance. Nor does it say how to build a better benchmark. Instead, behavioral finance suggests how to beat the

---

[5]By "the whole market," I don't mean every single stock; small-cap and value stocks were probably underpriced in the spring of 2000 and later rallied, whereas tech stocks were falling in 2000–2002. I mean that the overall level of broad, cap-weighted market benchmarks was too high.

benchmark (primarily but not entirely through value investing). Behavioral finance, moreover, does not overturn Sharpe's "arithmetic of active management"—the observation that the performances of all active managers in an asset class sum to the asset-class return. As a result, practitioners who subscribe to behavioral finance are charged with the same responsibility as any other active manager—beating the cap-weighted benchmark while managing active risk—and they are forced to do so by being smarter, more rational, or more immune to the seductions of greed and fear than their competitors.

Other Critiques of MPT. Other critiques of MPT that are not specifically aimed at benchmarking or the integrity of specific benchmarks but that bear on benchmarks in some way include the following:

- the allegation that MPT is invalid because it is based on unrealistic assumptions,
- the concern that optimizers are "error maximizers" and give unstable or unreliable results,
- the suggestion that standard deviation does not measure the real risk to which investors are averse, and
- the idea that riskier assets do not really have a higher expected rate of return than safe assets.

In Chapter 3, where I suggested that optimization is the right framework for thinking about manager selection and allocation, I introduced one of these criticisms—the "Michaud critique" (see Michaud 1998, 2003; Michaud and Michaud 2003)—and mentioned a response by Kritzman (2003). This section provides a brief description of the other three critiques.

■ *Unrealistic assumptions.* Portfolio theory is not intended to be realistic. Its assumptions—which include, for the CAPM, that all investors have equal and costless access to information and equal ability to process it—do not come close to describing the real world. Such a critique is not fair, however, because no theory is based on entirely realistic assumptions. The purpose of a theoretical model is to simplify reality enough that it can be analyzed, not to replicate reality in its every detail.

The challenge for those who would overturn a given theory is to propose a better theory. Despite great effort, and the promise of great reward to those who can solve the riddle of the markets better than Markowitz, Sharpe, and their fellows, nothing distinctive has emerged. The closest to an alternative theory is behavioral finance, but most of the advocates of behavioral finance do not think they have overturned MPT; their work does not propose a different way to construct benchmarks, nor does it (usually) propose to get rid of them.[6] But behaviorists have enriched the story of modern finance, making it more realistic and less dependent on fanciful assumptions, and they have suggested ways of beating existing benchmarks.

▪ *Standard deviation not a perfect measure of risk.* In fact, standard deviation doesn't quite capture the risk to which investors are, or should be, averse.[7] Sortino and Satchell (2001) suggested that semideviation—a measure like standard deviation that takes account only of observations below a target, or investor-specified minimum acceptable return—is a better measure than standard deviation because investors, presumably, aren't averse to good returns (which nevertheless contribute to standard deviation and thus to "risk" as conventionally measured). Other authors have suggested using deviation below the asset's own mean return.[8] Leibowitz and Henriksson (1989) proposed shortfall risk as a measure of the risk to which investors are averse; shortfall risk is the likelihood of a shortfall (expressed as a probability) multiplied by the expected severity of the shortfall should one occur.[9]

If you believe that a particular statistical measure, such as semideviation or shortfall risk, captures risk better than the traditional standard deviation measure does, then use it. Doing so does not affect the decision to use benchmarks or the decision as to which benchmark to use for a given portfolio or asset class. It does, however, affect performance measurement (because you are now defining good performance as alpha minus a penalty for *downside* active risk, or active *shortfall* risk, rather than for omega, active standard deviation; see Chapter 2). Many consultants, managers, and plan sponsors already use downside or shortfall measures of risk as well as the conventional standard deviation–based measures to calculate their performance statistics. Moreover, active managers who use quantitative methods to manage their tracking error should use a risk model that captures downside active risk or active shortfall risk if they believe such risk measures to be relevant.

---

[6]The use of an "absolute return benchmark" or "liability benchmark," discussed in Chapter 6, is sometimes advocated by the same people who criticize MPT or who say the market is not efficient. These alternative benchmarks (if you want to call them that) do not, however, fall directly out of the theoretical contributions made by critics of MPT and efficient markets. They are simply alternatives to conventional practice.

[7]Markowitz used standard deviation as the measure of risk because it makes the math notably easier than does any other risk measure, not because he thought it was the best measure that could be imagined.

[8]Markowitz himself acknowledged (1991) the potential value of semideviation below a target or below the asset's own mean as a measure of risk.

[9]By "shortfall" is meant a return below some minimum acceptable return or target.

■ *No return premium for riskier assets.* A more profound (but, in my view, extremely unpromising) challenge to MPT is the suggestion by Haugen (and others) that risk is not even positively related to expected return. Analyzing work done previously by Fama and French (1992), Haugen wrote:

> Within the largest stocks, those with the highest risk tend to have the lowest returns. The line of the best fit . . . has a negative slope. The same is true for the smallest stocks. High risk, low return. (1995, p. 97)

Behaviorists, who tend to be less radical than Haugen, have offered some support for this challenge to traditional finance. Shefrin, for example, in analyzing stated investor views (rather than past market results), wrote:

> [E]ven though investors may state that in principle, risk and expected return are positively related, in practice they form judgments in which the two are negatively related. (2002, pp. xxx–xxxi)[10]

If risk is unrelated to return on an aggregate level—that is, summing across all investors (or at least across price-setting investors) and looking among as well as within asset classes—the whole edifice of finance crumbles. The structures that fail include not only mean–variance optimization and the CAPM but also the pricing of corporate credit, performance measurement and evaluation, and risk management. That such a radical revision of finance is needed to explain observed phenomena is highly unlikely.

Conclusion

The bubble period of 1998–2000 embodied the crisis (in Kuhn's terminology) in MPT thinking that had been developing over the decades since the theory was first set forth by Markowitz and Sharpe. The crisis was resolved not by the introduction of a new theory that better fit the observed phenomena but, in a compromise, by a growing interest in behavioral considerations and by a better understanding of what MPT, benchmarks, and benchmarking are supposed to accomplish and what their limitations are.

---

[10]See also Shefrin (2001). Shefrin, like Haugen, was comparing riskier and safer *stocks* (not asset classes).

6. Critiques of Benchmarking and a Way Forward

In Chapter 2, I made the strong-form case for benchmarking (although not for indexing—I will never argue that active management is useless). Now, you will hear from the other side, and then I will propose a compromise.

Critiques of Benchmarking

Behavioral finance offers a critique of efficient markets, and thus of indexing, but not of benchmarking in the broader sense of using benchmarks for performance evaluation and active risk management. Other critiques, however, do target benchmarking. "Tracking error is supposed to be as large as possible, only positive," a traditional active manager recently told me. He was only partly kidding. One school of thought in the active management community, especially in the hedge fund world, contends that "real men" don't use cap-weighted market benchmarks as the starting point for portfolio construction.

According to this view, the risk is in buying the benchmark, not in deviating from it. You should be focused on avoiding real risk and on making money or, if you are a conservative investor, on preserving capital. You should not take real risk to avoid apparent risk (or to manage your business risk). This view considers "investing" to consist of analyzing securities and buying those that you believe will go up, not those that are popular with others and that have, therefore, already gone up, which causes them to have a large weight in cap-weighted benchmarks.

This approach is simply pre-MPT thinking with a contrarian cast and a value bias. The portfolios built by the advocates of this point of view are often more or less equally weighted and contain short positions as well as long ones (if, as in a hedge fund, short selling is permitted).

At stress points in the system—the spring of 2000 was one—the critiques of benchmarking resonate with almost everyone, and investors would have been well advised to listen to them that spring, and for a year or so before and after. On average across time, however, prices are at least somewhat related to fundamental value, which places the burden of proof clearly on those who imply, by poking fun at benchmarks, that they can easily beat them—and that they can do so at tolerable levels of active risk.

Critiques of Specific Benchmarks

Some critics of benchmarking are opposed to it not so much in principle but because of perceived shortcomings in widely used benchmarks. One such potential shortcoming is the decision process used to construct, or "manage," the S&P 500 Index, which is by far the most widely used U.S. equity benchmark. I focus on that issue in this section. Other issues relating to specific benchmarks include inclusion and deletion effects (which are a type of transaction cost) and high levels of turnover concentrated in a short time period. A case in point is the annual 30 June reconstitution of the Russell indexes, producer of "Russell mania." These issues are covered in Chapter 7. Disagreement about how to classify stocks into styles is also a crucial issue in indexing and benchmarking and is treated in Chapter 8. In Chapters 9–11, I discuss the concern that benchmarks in asset classes other than U.S. equity are misleading or poorly constructed.

Is the S&P 500 Managed? In a kind of mirror image of the critique that the S&P 500 is a poor portfolio to hold because it is stuffed with overpriced stocks, some managers and clients have expressed frustration that the S&P 500 is a difficult index to beat (or to track) because it is "actively managed" through the process by which Standard & Poor's decides what stocks should be in the index at a given time.

My first reaction to this allegation is surprise. Most active managers fail to add any alpha relative to their benchmarks if measured over a long time period. Why should Standard & Poor's be any better at active management than those who practice it with real money?[1] Rattray and Manglani (2003) found, however, that the S&P 500 did, in fact, beat a purely rule-based, passive benchmark (the "top 500" U.S. stocks by capitalization, reranked and rebalanced monthly) by 0.26 percentage points (pps) a year over the 1992–2002 period.[2] The tracking error between the two indexes was a nontrivial 2.08 percent a year. These authors found that the outperformance arose from a value bias (value beat growth in 1992–2002 by a large margin), largely caused by Standard & Poor's unusual requirement that companies have four quarters

---

[1]In equities, Standard & Poor's is simply an index constructor, not an asset manager. Standard & Poor's also provides "ratings" (credit assessments) of fixed-income securities.

[2]Rattray and Manglani used the same definition of "U.S. stocks" that Standard & Poor's did at each point in time, so their "top 500" sometimes included American Depositary Receipts and sometimes did not. This approach isolates the effect of the S&P decision rules and discretionary calls on the relative returns of the two indexes.

of profitability to be selected for the index.[3] Because of the profitability requirement and because Standard & Poor's tries to achieve "sector balance," technology stocks were underrepresented in the S&P 500 relative to the Top 500. This technology underrepresentation helped in 2000–2002 more than it hurt in 1998–1999.

Digging further, Rattray and Manglani found that, after they adjusted for the impact of the profitability rule and other fixed rules, the pure stock-selection skill of the S&P 500 committee was *negative.* In other words, Standard & Poor's "discretionary application of the rules" rather than the rules themselves reduced returns by about 0.11 pps annually. This finding is reassuring, especially for anyone who has tried to beat the S&P 500 through active stock selection.

These performance numbers are before adjusting for the S&P 500 inclusion (or reconstitution) effect—that is, the material rise in the price of a stock between the date of the announcement that it will be added to the S&P 500 and the date the stock is actually added to the index. If you assume you could have bought the stocks at the closing price on the day of the announcement—which makes the S&P 500 directly comparable to the Top 500 strategy because the Top 500 was not a real portfolio and had no inclusion effect—the S&P 500 did even better, with a 0.58 pp a year advantage over the Top 500.[4]

The S&P 500, then, is indeed an actively managed portfolio. Before transaction costs, Standard & Poor's has added some alpha. This alpha may or may not be repeatable; it is certainly not statistically significant (the alpha *t*-statistic for 1992–2002 is 0.92). After transaction costs, the alpha is limited to a weak value effect caused by the profitability requirement and perhaps by limits on sector weights. To be safe, you might do better to benchmark your portfolio to a purely rule-based index rather than to the S&P 500.

Is S&P 500 Outperformance a Momentum Effect? The S&P 500's outperformance could be a momentum effect and could represent evidence that the index is distorting the market. If so, the outperformance would have been concentrated in the up-market years of 1995–1999 and would have reversed during the bear market of 2000–2002. In fact, however, the outperformance was strongest in 2000 and did not vary significantly between up and down markets in general. So, the outperformance is a value, not a momentum, effect. Moreover, Rattray and Manglani's study contains no evidence that indexing to the S&P 500 causes distorted markets.

---

[3] Once in the S&P 500, however, companies that become unprofitable are not deleted except under extreme circumstances.

[4] I provide more detail on the Standard & Poor's inclusion effect in the Chapter 7 discussion of index price distortions.

Reaction

In a trend reflective of the critiques of benchmarking, some of the habits of mind grounded in the original pre-MPT paradigm are making a comeback. The most prominent is the desire to earn an "absolute" return, a return independent of what the markets are doing. How this goal is attainable on any large scale is not clear: The beta of all portfolios must average to one, not zero.[5] On a limited scale, however, investors can hold balanced short and long positions or simply select securities or time the market with the intent of earning a return uncorrelated with either the stock or the bond market. Such investments (which are usually structured as hedge funds) are typically measured against an "absolute return benchmark."

Investing in balanced long–short positions is a legitimate investment strategy. What troubles me is the use of a so-called absolute return benchmark. Typical absolute return benchmarks are "Treasury bills plus 5 percent" or "inflation plus 5 percent" (which often represents the spending goals or requirements of an endowment fund or foundation). But a good benchmark is generally one for which an index fund or tracking portfolio can be constructed. Because no asset other than cash pays an absolute return, very little information can be gained from comparing a portfolio with an absolute return benchmark.

Moreover, I am not optimistic that efforts to earn an absolute return (above that of cash) can succeed, even on a limited scale, more often than would be predicted by chance—although if you did succeed, the rewards would be spectacular.[6] There is a great deal of active risk involved in so-called absolute return investing, and you should be cautious when confronted with a manager who takes the position that "I'm so smart, the usual rules (benchmarks) don't apply to me!" But the current level of interest in absolute return investing is so intense, and the arguments applied by those who advocate it so persuasive on their face, that I devote some attention to this view of the world. And I will argue that one kind of alternative benchmark does make sense for many, if not most, institutions or asset pools—a benchmark that represents the return on the institution's *liabilities*. A focus on liabilities, not on absolute return benchmarks, is the key contribution being made by those who are skeptical of the traditional approach to benchmarking.

---

[5]If all portfolios were hedge funds, their aggregate beta would also be 1.0.

[6]Rewards would be fantastic not only in terms of investment performance but also with regard to the fees that could be collected.

A Perspective from Peter Bernstein

Peter Bernstein, the best-selling author of *Against the Gods* and many other works, is a particularly eloquent advocate of the point of view that you ought to operate in a way that is basically unconstrained by benchmarks, at both the policy and manager levels. Unlike most advocates of benchmark-independent investing, who are merely making self-interested arguments to bolster their case for a large active-risk budget or a fat fee, Bernstein is an independent observer of markets whose views are almost universally respected.[7] His career spans more than half a century. With his permission, this section quotes him at length.[8] After presenting his point of view, I will make suggestions toward a compromise.

Bernstein began by assuming that active management is not a complete waste of time and money:

> I must mention at the outset that the whole structure depends on one overarching assumption—that clients can identify managers capable of generating alphas. (p. 1)[9]

He then argued at length that "traditional benchmarking for active portfolio managers is contrary to the client's best interest" (p. 4) because capitalization-weighted benchmarks are heavily weighted in the currently "hot" stocks and because managers are in a horse race with no well-defined track and a constantly moving finish line. He then defined an investment environment free of traditional benchmarks:

> It must be to the client's best interest to maximize the alphas they are capable of generating. Yet alpha is a relative term, not an absolute one. If we free up the manager from the constraints of the traditional benchmark, how can we discover whether any alpha has been created? How do we make a judgment about a manager's performance?
>
> The answer . . . is that we cannot make judgments in the traditional manner. The data that emerge from the traditional process are not meaningless—I do not mean to go that far—but they create difficulties for clients because they are constraining. (p. 4)

If you are selecting managers with real skill, the kind to whom (as I said in the Preface) traditional benchmarks are shackles, how should you measure performance? Bernstein wrote:

> I propose that client start at the beginning and move forward. The beginning is the determination of the required return of the total portfolio and the degree of volatility that client can live with in the search for that required return.

---

[7]By "independent," I mean that he does not, as far as I know, manage any investments for others.

[8]All the quotations that follow are from Bernstein's "A Modest Proposal: Portfolio Management Practice for Modern Times" (2000).

[9]See also Waring and Siegel (2003).

When it comes to defining benchmarks, *faute de mieux* the riskless rate itself can serve the purpose, with the active portfolio built up from there. One can go further, however, with the required return falling out of a careful specification of investment objectives. For example, most foundations seek inflation plus 5 percent, pension funds could use as a benchmark an immunized portfolio with zero tracking error to the fund's liability return, endowment funds take spending rates as the key to required returns, and individuals would do well to begin to think of their own objectives in similar kinds of frameworks. (p. 5)

But what does a liability-focused benchmark mean in practice?

The proper question to ask about an active management organization is not whether it is beating the S&P 500, the Lehman . . . or its peer group. The question should be: How much is this organization contributing to a return in excess of our required return, and at what level of volatility? A manager with bond-like returns but equity-like volatility gets fired; a manager with equity-like returns and bond-like volatility receives an increased allocation. I admit that this keeps the old horse race running, but at least the track and finish line are properly defined. (p. 5)

The consequences of using such a framework for performance measurement, in Bernstein's view, include the following:

- a much looser set of marching orders for managers,
- greater "breadth" in the uses to which a given set of active management skills are put,[10]
- larger allocations to managers who are not afraid to be, in Kritzman's (1998) words, "wrong and alone,"
- greater use of large, multistrategy organizations, and
- greater responsibility on the part of the client's investment officer.

Bernstein acknowledged that his prescription might result in reduced diversification:

With widened mandates, the possibility exists that all the domestic equity managers will run to [international] investments at the same moment, or all desert one or another subdivisions of the domestic market. (p. 7)

He had concluded, however, that if implemented sensibly, an investment policy that is focused on seeking return relative to a liability benchmark (or simply an absolute rate of return) and avoiding absolute risk (which he defined as volatility) can "circumvent to the extent possible the dangerous conflicts of interest in traditional arrangements that fester between manager's risk and owner's risk" (p. 7).

---

[10]In their Chapter 5, Grinold and Kahn (2000) defined "breadth" as the number of unrelated investment decisions a manager has the freedom to make. They also proposed the following "fundamental law of active management": At a given level of skill, investment performance is proportional to breadth as defined in this way.

Toward a Compromise

How can Bernstein's views be reconciled with the position I took in Chapter 2 that alpha and active return (measured in relation to a properly selected and constructed benchmark) are the only things that matter? It can't, but as promised, I can outline the structure of a potential compromise. A sponsor's attitude toward active management and managers might be as follows:

- We believe in the abstract that superior managers exist, but we're from Missouri and you'll have to show us. We're going to continue to measure, AND PAY, you (as described in Chapter 3) by "pure" alpha, active risk, and information ratio.

- However, it's rational and potentially fruitful to spend some of our risk budget on managers who are a little different from the crowd, who even may not fit into a single asset class, much less a style. We'll hold them to active return–active risk standards also, and we'll construct a benchmark for them. It could conceivably be a liability-focused benchmark, but more likely, the benchmark will be composed of the returns on the asset class or classes in which we believe the manager is likely to invest.

- At the policy level, we will establish a policy benchmark, but we will not be afraid to stray from it. We're going to compare our own actual asset-class mix with that of the policy benchmark, and we'll calculate our information ratio—pure alpha per unit of tracking error. (Plan sponsors shouldn't be scared of this measurement protocol. The rewards from being right about asset allocation are so generous that any skill in making them will be evident from an information ratio perspective.)

- If we think a traditional active manager's active bets are so unlikely to be successful that we feel we have to hold them to a strict tracking-error constraint, we won't hire them. We will hire managers in whom we have confidence instead, and although we'll measure their tracking error to a sensible benchmark and count that against their risk budgets, we won't constrain them. We'll let the managers do what they want, and we'll let them do their own constraining by being forced to generate information ratio, not just alpha. Thus, although tracking-error constraints are a flawed construct, we are still averse to tracking error. In short, measuring tracking error and rewarding the manager for information ratio is still a good idea.

- We are very much concerned about costs (including manager fees and indirect costs, such as trading costs.). Costs are the one dimension of investment management that can be controlled, so index funds and other low-cost funds have a special place.

If you work through this framework to generate an investment policy, you will wind up with larger-than-traditional weights on index funds, enhanced index funds, and certain types of hedge funds (those that control risk and that deliver pure alpha, not beta masquerading as alpha). You may also make increased use of balanced (including global balanced) funds and tactical asset allocation funds. This framework provides only a small role for traditional active managers benchmarked to a narrowly defined style. Given the huge cluster of resources currently deployed in traditional active management, however, the investor would be derelict to avoid it completely.

No one really knows (yet) how to follow Bernstein's prescription literally. (I lay out further thoughts on it in the discussion of policy benchmarks in Chapter 12.) What he defines as active risk may be too much influenced by luck to provide a realistic assessment of a manager's skill. Using Bernstein's standard, a large indexed position in the equity market in 1995–1999 would have been scored as a huge active win; if the objective is, say, to earn inflation plus 5 percent, then earning inflation plus 15 percent on a consistent basis for several years should indeed be scored as a win. But without gathering additional information, it is impossible to tell whether investors who had such a position did so because they thought it would earn the highest possible return after adjusting for risk or because all of their peers were doing it. If the spur was peer pressure, the position was not a win but a stroke of luck (that is, the investor had no skill) and much of the gain from holding it would have unwound by the end of 2002 because the investor, like his or her peers, would have remained invested in the stock market. Real skill must be quantifiable, and if new technologies are needed to measure it in today's supposedly new investment climate, then the search should be on to develop them.

Conclusion

Despite the challenges to benchmarking, and to cap-weighted benchmarks in particular, that have arisen in the past decade, cap-weighted benchmarks will continue to have a special place in investment management and analysis for a simple reason: *You can't design a simple, rule-based, judgment-free portfolio that is demonstrably more efficient than the cap-weighted benchmark.*

Some people have suggested equal-weighted benchmarks, book-value- or earnings-weighted benchmarks, and other types (such as international equity benchmarks that are weighted by gross domestic product by country).[11] But except for equally weighted portfolios, proponents of these alternatives cannot even agree on sensible rules for constructing such benchmarks, much less prove that these portfolios are more efficient than a cap-weighted one (and equally weighted portfolios have very limited capacity).[12] Finally, a theory exists—the capital asset pricing model, with all its flaws—that says cap-weighted benchmarks are efficient. No theory exists—not even a proposed and untested one—that says some other simple, rule-based portfolio is efficient. As a result of all these factors, benchmarking relative to cap-weighted indexes as an important component of a broader performance-measurement discipline (one that also includes comparison with liability-focused benchmarks) is probably here to stay.

---

[11]A definitive examination of the efficiency of equally weighted portfolios is that of Jobson and Korkie (1981). They found that in some conditions, an equally weighted portfolio is as efficient as, or even more efficient than, a cap-weighted one. The small-cap effect, which was powerful in the time period leading up to Jobson and Korkie's work, may at least partly explain this result. If that effect is the correct explanation, their results will not be repeatable.

[12]Another line of reasoning about benchmarks is represented by Haugen (1995), who constructed an "efficient index" based on optimization that used estimates of security returns, risks, and correlations derived from fundamental factors. I believe this approach is simply active management: An investor who does not have access to Haugen's specific forecasts cannot determine what the benchmark contents will be.

7. The Impact of Benchmarking on Markets and Institutions

Many observers have suggested that indexing and benchmarking have distorting effects on market prices and on the behavior of institutions. (Keep in mind that by "benchmarking," I mean active management that uses a cap-weighted index, or benchmark, as a starting point and that defines active risk as tracking error relative to the benchmark.) In this chapter, I examine these distortions. The distortions of market pricing that are alleged to accompany indexing and benchmarking may be classified into micro and macro categories. "Micro" distortions generally mean mispricings of one security relative to another; such mispricings tend to be either small but potentially long lasting or potentially large but temporary. These distortions tend to be self-correcting in the long run, but that aspect does not make them trivial. Having to persistently overpay for a class of securities, for example, or having to accept an unfairly low price when selling them, may have a significant effect on an investor's long-term returns.

"Macro" distortions, in contrast, are those that have potentially pervasive and long-lasting effects on market levels or on the level of a significant subset of the market. These distortions emerge because, as noted in the conceptual critique discussed in Chapter 5, by holding the benchmark, the investor is doing what everybody else is doing (because the benchmark is the cap-weighted sum of all prices). Thus, indexing and benchmarking are, according to this critique, a form of herd behavior. I explore the consequences of this observation in discussing the impact of benchmarking on institutions, but such an exploration must be more speculative than the treatment of micro distortions because practically no data are available on the macro side.

I also discuss the effect of indexing and of active management (of the kind in which risk is defined as tracking error) on the behavior of such institutions as plan sponsors and their governing committees, investment management firms, consulting firms, and plan beneficiaries.

Market Price Distortions

Observed micro effects on prices include a number of different index reconstitution effects. In addition, free-float mismatch is a micro distortion that has received increasing attention recently.

S&P 500 Index Reconstitution Effect. The first indexers never dreamed that their activities would move market prices, but an "S&P 500 inclusion effect" nevertheless quickly emerged. The inclusion effect is that stocks added to the S&P 500 rise in price dramatically upon announcement of their addition to the index as all the index fund managers try to add the stock to their portfolios at the lowest possible cost. Stocks deleted from the index suffer a corresponding price decline.

Such an effect probably exists with respect to all indexes that have substantial assets under index fund management, although it is presumably smaller for indexes other than the S&P 500. Index funds that track rule-based indexes with predictable constituent changes should have a much less pronounced cost disadvantage from the inclusion effect because investors can act in advance of the changes.

The reason for the inclusion and deletion effects (classified together as a reconstitution effect) is obvious: An increase in the demand for a stock caused by the need for index funds to hold that stock is not met by any change in supply. Thus, the price rises. The market clears when active managers and arbitrageurs, motivated by the desire to sell stocks that have gone up, provide indexers with enough of the stock to enable them to hold it in exactly the index weight.[1] The deletion effect is simply the mirror image of the inclusion effect. The inflexibility of index fund design (a virtue from some points of view) makes reconstitution effects inevitable.

One can interpret reconstitution-related price movements in either of two ways. The price-pressure hypothesis holds that "transitory order imbalance[s] associated with index additions and deletions are the primary source of price movements" (Madhavan 2002, p. 3). The index membership hypothesis holds that index membership itself is a source of value (because of greater liquidity or better information flow), so an inclusion effect is permanent rather than transitory. The two hypotheses are not mutually exclusive; both effects could exist.

The first works that identified the S&P 500 reconstitution effect are Goetzmann and Garry (1986), Harris and Gurel (1986), and Jain (1987). Although somewhat out of date, these studies convey the essence of the effect. Harris and Gurel found excess returns on the announcement day of 3.1 percentage points (pps) for additions and −1.4 pps for deletions, in addition to large trading volumes. They interpreted these results as the effects of transitory price pressure. The Goetzmann–Garry and Jain studies found persistent,

---

[1] The major categories of arbitrageurs are (1) hedge funds and (2) the proprietary trading desks of brokerage firms.

long-term stock price declines upon deletion of a stock from the S&P 500. Thus, evidence supporting both the price-pressure and index-membership hypotheses exists.

The implication of these results is that, relative to an idealized situation of no reconstitution effects, the investor overpays for index funds and receives too little. One author's estimate of S&P 500 underperformance as a result of the inclusion/deletion effects in recent years (expressed as an annual rate) is 0.32 pps for 1992–2002 (see Chapter 6). The amount of underperformance has, of course, been increasing as indexed assets have grown.

After paying the transaction cost caused by the inclusion/deletion effects, an investor in an index fund does, of course, receive the asset-class or style return almost for free because index funds have low management fees. It is up to the investor to decide if this trade-off is worthwhile.

■ *Smart trading.* Some index managers put a great deal of effort into trading disciplines that avoid these reconstitution costs to the greatest extent possible. Such "smart trading" tends to reduce the costs of all transacting, not only costs associated with index reconstitution. Moreover, because firms managing large index funds are *providers* (not just consumers) of liquidity, they may even be able to turn the tables on the arbitrageurs and capture for their investors some of the liquidity premium traditionally received by the "arbs." Managers who are successful at this endeavor can beat the index (by a modest amount) without making any active bets.[2]

■ *Reconstitution effect from active management.* Inclusion/deletion effects are probably also caused by benchmark-sensitive management of actively managed portfolios, but these effects cannot be observed separately. As I noted previously, ordinary active managers and self-conscious arbitrageurs provide some of the liquidity needed to effect index funds' reconstitution-related trades and thus profit from the reconstitution. By and large, however, active managers are probably paying, not receiving, reconstitution-related costs. Here is the logic: When a stock is added to an index, the demand from active managers for that stock must increase in roughly the same proportion as the demand from indexers because, on average, the managers will hold the index weight. The reason this effect is not plainly observed is that each manager individually has wide discretion as to whether to hold the stock and how to time the purchase. Moreover, active managers have a strong motivation to avoid paying such unnecessary transaction costs, and now that a reconstitution effect has been identified, at least some active managers have found a way to dodge these costs.

---

[2]Because the index is calculated on a basis that assumes reconstitution-related costs have been paid, strategies that reduce these costs are seen as adding alpha.

Thus, although some of the overall observed reconstitution effect probably comes from active managers' demand, it is muted, and some active managers profit from the effect while others are hurt by it.

Russell Mania. A market microstructure effect that is closely related to but somewhat different in character from the S&P reconstitution effect is what has come to be called "Russell mania." It might seem that the Russell reconstitution, which occurs every 30 June, would be relatively free of price distortions and other technical effects because it is based purely on market capitalization, which is observable by all interested parties in real time. Madhavan found, however:

> Equity returns [arising from the reconstitution of the Russell 3000 and its subindexes] are concentrated in time and are much larger in magnitude and in the number of stocks affected than the corresponding effects for S&P 500 index revisions. Specifically, a portfolio long additions and short deletions to the Russell 3000 index (constructed after the determination of new index weights at the end of May) had a mean return over the period 1996–2001 of 15 percent in the month of June. From March–June, the cumulative mean return exceeds 35 percent. (2002, p. 1)

These numbers are *huge*. Understandably, index funds, active managers, hedge funds, brokers, and others find themselves in an annual mania—to capture such returns if they are the liquidity providers and to avoid paying them as a cost if they are the liquidity consumers.

One reason for this large effect is that stocks being added to the Russell 3000 (which embraces 98 percent of U.S. equity market value) are tiny, so they are disproportionately affected by either transitory or permanent changes in demand. An odd institutional artifact, however, makes the Russell effect more complicated and more fun for arbitrageurs. Most large-cap portfolios are indexed or benchmarked to the S&P 500, not the Russell 1000, but a sizable chunk of small-cap portfolios is indexed or benchmarked to the Russell 2000. Thus, when a stock moves from the Russell 1000 to the Russell 2000, because its relative market cap has declined, the demand for the stock *increases*.[3]

Free-Float Mismatch: The "Yahoo! Effect." The most dramatic S&P 500 inclusion effect in history occurred on 7 December 1999, the day before Yahoo! was added to that index (replacing Laidlaw, the largest school-bus company). On that day, the price of Yahoo! rose by $67.25 per share, or 24 percent, to close at $348, as 66 million shares changed hands. Previously, from

---

[3]The effects of index reconstitutions on international equity prices are discussed in Chapter 10. To make sense of the evidence on international reconstitution effects, a reader must first understand in some detail how international equity indexes are constructed, particularly as regards float adjustment and inclusion/deletion of countries.

the announcement on 30 November 1999 that Yahoo! would be included in the S&P 500 to the inclusion date, investors had run up the stock by 32 percent. This mysterious price levitation was not the result of any special enthusiasm for Yahoo! stock (Yahoo! was just another constituent of the S&P index, and its special merits, whatever they were, were not under consideration that day). The cause was the fact that Yahoo! had been added to the S&P 500 at its full market-cap weight without any adjustment for the free float (the number of shares held by stockholders who were at liberty to sell). Because most shares were held by employees, venture capital firms, and other investors who were restricted from selling, the true supply of Yahoo! shares was only about 10 percent of the full market cap. The result was the radical supply–demand imbalance manifest in the price spike.

The situation was mitigated by the fact that only about 8 percent of the capitalization of the S&P 500 is in index funds linked to the S&P 500. Thus, the demand as well as the supply was limited. If a much larger proportion of the capitalization of the S&P 500 had been in S&P 500 indexed funds, the index fund demand for Yahoo! might not have been met at any price. The market has no precedent for a stock having an infinite price, so, surely, the Micawber rule ("Something will turn up") would have prevailed.[4] Restricted stockholders might have found a way around the restrictions, someone might have issued derivatives acceptable to the index funds, or the funds might have forced Standard & Poor's to drop Yahoo! from the index.

At any rate, the importance of float adjustment, which was previously thought by many to be an unnecessary (or even undesirable) complication in index construction, suddenly became clear. Yahoo! was far from the only stock that was eventually affected; many of the emerging technology companies had little free float because of the need to compensate employees and venture capitalists with restricted stock. Float-adjusted indexes increased in popularity, and Morgan Stanley Capital International converted to a float-adjusted format not long after the Yahoo! episode, although MSCI's action was primarily for other reasons (see Chapter 10).

Games Hedge Funds Play. Today, for the first time, much of the market's liquidity is provided by hedge funds—entrepreneurial, risk-seeking, and often highly leveraged institutions that are typically accountable to no one other than their owner/investors. Hedge funds are so named for their original goal of "hedging" or reducing risk, but they more often take risks that investors constrained by traditional benchmarks are loath to accept (see Chapter 11). Brokerage houses, the traditional source of liquidity in the stock market, have a smaller role than they once did.

---

[4]Charles Dickens, *David Copperfield* (1849).

Hedge funds were not established to provide liquidity; they exist to make outsize profits by taking unusual risks. That they do provide liquidity is basically an unintended consequence of their operations (as well as a source of their returns). Index reconstitutions are a major consumer of the liquidity that hedge funds provide.

Thus, investors trading in anticipation of or in reaction to changes in index contents should be aware that, with a high degree of likelihood, they are buying from or selling to a hedge fund that may have better information and possibly greater influence over market prices than the investors do. Careful attention to trading disciplines is a good idea in all situations but especially in index reconstitutions, where demand is predictable and the other side of the trade can be presumed to have put great effort into forecasting it. Active managers as well as index fund managers can benefit from this observation.

Institutional Behavior

In this section, I describe two effects of benchmarking: the play-it-safe impact of benchmarking on active managers and the emergence of index funds as a major force in the market.

The Impact of Benchmarking on Active Managers. The first-order impact of benchmarking on managers (as opposed to markets) is simply to get active managers to take less active risk. Active managers cannot manage active risk if they have never heard of it, as in the original paradigm. Increased awareness from investors, consultants, and managers of the existence and nature of active risk has dramatically reduced the amount of active risk taken; up to 35 percent of the capitalization of U.S. equities is said to be indexed, and probably another 50 percent is managed with an explicit goal of managing active risk while seeking active return. This outcome is exactly as I argued it should be in Chapter 3. A smaller but significant proportion of international equities is indexed or benchmarked, as is a large proportion of fixed-income assets.

But if indexing and benchmarked active management are largely desirable outcomes, they still have a downside. First, as I noted at the outset, for those rare managers with true skill, the concern about active risk leads to impaired courage and, thereby, to lower returns. This result is sometimes described by frustrated managers as being forced to take "real" risk to avoid taking "apparent" risk. Second, probably a more important drawback, the ability to manage a portfolio in a benchmark-sensitive manner has enabled many managers with little or no real skill to deliver only market-like returns but, because of two decades of rising markets, to give their clients the impression that they have added value. And they've been able to charge active fees for this "service." It remains to be seen whether managers who deliver only beta exposures and no alpha (or little alpha per unit of active risk) can maintain their client bases in markets that fluctuate (instead of only going up). I hope not.

In addition, active managers have tightly clustered themselves into styles so that they can be classified into one of the consultants' style boxes. Most consultants and clients do not know how (or do not bother) to run the multivariate regressions described in Chapter 2; instead, they compare a manager's returns with the single style benchmark that seems to fit best. Thus, a manager has to stay within relatively tight style bounds to be hired by investors acting under their consultants' advice. This practice—which could be called "managing your business risk instead of your portfolio"—has not only restrained the taking of active risk relative to style benchmarks but also discouraged managers from trying to manage broad-cap or core portfolios, to time investments between styles or sectors, or to practice other tactical allocation disciplines—which are as good a way as any to try to add alpha.

The prescription that managers should seek only pure alpha and avoid only pure active risk relative to a properly style-adjusted benchmark does *not* mean that they should "hug" the style benchmarks. If a manager adopts a mix of styles or uses a timing approach to move between styles, the method outlined in Chapter 2 will capture the pure alpha and pure active risk correctly.

Emergence and Popularity of Index Funds. Increased awareness of benchmarks has also led to a vibrant index fund sector. Even proverbially naive individual investors are now more or less universally aware that index funds exist and have low management fees. They allocate to active funds because they think they can beat the index fund, not because they have been exposed only to opportunities for active investment. Index funds (and, to some extent, enhanced index funds, which start with the security weights in the benchmark and then try to add value through risk-controlled active management) now form the core of many, if not most, institutional equity portfolios. This state of affairs must have been a shock and a delight to the pioneers who developed the first index funds only a generation ago, most of whom are still active in the investment management business.

Many observers guess that the move in so short a time from indexing nothing to indexing something like 35 percent of all U.S. equities simply has to have had some effect on market levels and price discovery. I now examine several points of view on this question.

Macro Effects: How Much Indexing Is Too Much?

Ever since indexing started, speculation has occurred about how much indexing is too much. Logically, if everyone indexed all of their assets, no one would be left to price securities. The price-discovery process would disappear, and markets would be completely inefficient. No one seriously suggests that this eventuality can happen because the potential profits from security analysis would be huge. Ibbotson and Brinson (1987) referred to this idea as the "student's proof of market inefficiency" because, in the experience of finance professors, there is always a bright student in the introductory course who says, "If every investor believed that markets were efficient, the market could not be efficient because no one would analyze securities" (p. 58).[5]

The recent market bubble might have been a hint of what would happen if no one analyzed securities. If no one tried (very hard) to determine the fundamental values of, say, large-cap technology stocks but simply bought them because of their large weights in the benchmark—which is similar to saying that you are buying them because they have gone up—price would become quickly divorced from value.[6]

Taking this observation a bit further and applying it to markets in general, Arnott and Darnell wrote:

> Passive management is the ultimate momentum strategy. Passive investing puts the most money into the largest stocks—not the largest companies, but . . . the stocks that have been the most successful *in the past* and are the most expensive compared to their fundamentals *in the present*. (2003, p. 31; italics in original)

In other words, a lot of indexing may have made the market less efficient and (some would argue) made the cap-weighted market benchmark easier to beat through a fundamental valuation approach.

This situation *cannot* go on forever. Active management is still a zero-sum game and, as Arnott and Darnell noted, even the best managers have alphas that slowly regress to zero over very long time periods. Warren Buffett, perhaps the greatest manager ever, earned only a 0.7 information ratio over the past 33 years; his firm's IR was only 0.48 over the 20 years and 3 months ended March 2000. Arnott and Darnell noted that this IR is modest by the standards of plan sponsors looking at managers' three-year track records and self-assessments of their future prospects but "is sufficient to make [Buffett] the world's wealthiest investor (with his co-investors participating almost fully in these gains, contrary to many investment managers)" (p. 32).

Managers cannot win the zero-sum game over long time periods by contrarian investing relative to a cap-weighted benchmark. So, what should the investor do when the bubble is over, when valuation disparities between

---

[5]On pp. 57–59, Ibbotson and Brinson review other reasons the market cannot be perfectly efficient. See also Grossman and Stiglitz (1980).

[6]Now that the bubble is well behind us, it is a good time to look for really strained arguments from finance professors as to why prices during the bubble were actually rational.

styles and market sectors are no longer disturbingly large? Arnott and Darnell suggested (surprisingly and, I think, sensibly) a strange new respect for passive investing:

> Consider passive only when active managers have done considerably better than passive managers, lest we enter an up elevator just before it goes down. Consider passive only when a switch to passive will not involve selling our most sensibly priced stocks in order to buy the market's most expensive stocks. (p. 33)

There is not much literature in which researchers try to actually estimate from data the size of the macro effect of indexing. In general, disentangling all the effects at work is too difficult. William Jacques, however, in a 1988 article that superficially sounds like just another "S&P inclusion effect" paper, had the following to say about the consequences in the very long run of membership in that index over the period (1973–1987) when indexing and benchmarking first came to fruition:

> Stocks belonging to the S&P 500 produced approximately 4.0 percent per year of extra return [over 1980–1987], compared with non-index companies with similar characteristics. The phenomenon seems to be accelerating. . . . As active equity managers lost share to index funds, non-S&P 500 stocks were sold to make room for S&P 500 purchases. Not only was buying pressure placed on index members, but selling pressure was exerted in a less liquid sector of the market. (p. 73)

A 4 percent a year cumulative excess return over eight years amounts to almost 37 percent. Jacques' conclusions—that a very large segment of the market became 37 percent more expensive relative to the rest of the market—is qualitatively different from the findings discussed earlier in the section on the S&P inclusion effect and should be regarded as evidence of a macro effect from indexing and benchmarking.

Jacques noted that the cumulative excess return to S&P 500 membership began around 1979, just when the indexing ball got rolling. Regarding benchmarking, Jacques noted that "a more subtle version of buying pressure on the S&P 500 members was generated during the 1980s by closet indexers . . . [namely] those institutional investors who feel compelled to construct portfolios whose results will be unlikely to deviate much from the . . . index" (p. 73).

Of course, the view that indexing can cause price distortions on a macro scale is not universally accepted. Rex Sinquefield, an index fund pioneer, enunciated quite a different view. His arguments are heterodox and fascinating:

> If there were a tremendous amount of indexing, it would not necessarily affect the accuracy of prices. As Adam Smith and Friedrich Hayek were quick to point out, we really don't know how the price discovery process works. So to say that indexed assets won't contribute to price discovery means that one believes price discovery relies specifically on equity analysts. I'm not sure of that at all.

Take, for example, the days before stock markets, when we had goods and services markets around the world for hundreds or thousands of years. Adam Smith and others show that these markets basically work and that civilizations based on free market prices survived, while those that didn't use markets to price goods and services did not survive. We did not have equity analysts back then; we just had people competing in the marketplace providing market pressures to keep prices in line relative to all the alternative consumption and service items that could be bought or sold.

Now taking into consideration stocks and other financial assets in the U.S., there are agents that (regardless of the amount indexed) would always have an interest in keeping prices right or at least in evaluating the prices. Company managements themselves do this when they undertake a "make or buy" decision—should we expand, contract, buy a competitor, should someone buy us, or should we just buy real resources and expand that way? The company's management is comparing the prices of their company, their competitors, and real resources, and this process tends to keep each of these prices in line with the underlying real economic worth of the assets being considered. Market makers, in addition, are always going to have some sense of the valuations of companies. Those are just two sources of price discovery in a highly indexed world.[7]

I suspect that, at the current level of indexing and benchmarking, the macro effect of these practices is sufficient to exacerbate bubbles and crashes considerably. In other words, indexing and benchmarking create price-discovery problems when conditions are extreme.

But modern markets have not experienced many episodes like the bubble of 1998–2000 and the subsequent bear market (the only truly comparable valuations at the peak were in 1929 in the United States and 1989 in Japan). Usually, prices are more sensible. In more ordinary times, indexing and benchmarking probably do not make the market very inefficient. If the momentum strategy argument against indexing is generalizable across time, then value investing should have been a better strategy in the indexing era (say, after 1980) than it was when there were no index funds or almost no assets in index funds. As you will see in Chapter 8, no such pattern emerges. The returns to value and growth investing seesawed back and forth, with value retaining a long-term advantage, in both the pre-indexing and indexing eras.

If the market is inefficient on a large scale because of indexing or some other reason, highly skilled analysts should be able to earn outsize returns at the expense of the less skilled. There is little evidence to indicate that many of them can do so consistently over long periods of time. The market is, at the very least, efficient enough to humble most of us.

---

[7]Personal communication.

8. U.S. Equity Style Indexes

Equity "style" is an elusive and challenging concept.[1] Investors and researchers have long noticed that stock returns tend to cluster (Sharpe 1970; Rosenberg 1974)—in other words, stock returns have factors in common other than the market factor. If they do, a sensible approach is to try to aggregate equities at a level intermediate between the whole market at the macro end and industries and other small groups at the micro end. The construct known as "investment style" is the result of that effort.

Beginning in the late 1970s, researchers noted that two factors—capitalization and valuation—explained a great deal of the cross-section of stock returns. By "capitalization" I mean the fact that small-cap stocks behave differently from large-cap stocks. By "valuation" I mean that stocks selling for low multiples of earnings, book value, or other related fundamental measures behave differently from those selling for high multiples. The low-multiple stocks are the so-called value stocks, and the high-multiple stocks are the growth stocks (because higher-than-average rates of growth are needed to justify the higher multiples).[2]

Prior to the discovery of the capitalization and valuation effects, the capital asset pricing model (CAPM, see Chapter 4) had related the returns on stocks to that on the overall market—that is, to a single factor. And Barr Rosenberg and others had made progress in relating stock returns to multiple factors. The identification of size and valuation—two easily described and easily measured factors—however, enabled consultants and their investor clients to classify stocks, categorize managers, and build style benchmarks in a systematic and meaningful way.

---

[1]Portions of this chapter also appeared in Pope, Rakvin, and Platt (2003), of which I was a contributing editor. I thank Theodore R. Aronson of Aronson+Johnson+Ortiz, Clifford S. Asness of AQR Capital Management, and Paul D. Kaplan of Morningstar for valuable discussions over the years about value and growth investing and many other topics.

[2]When the capitalization and valuation effects were discovered in the late 1970s, they were widely regarded as ways to beat the market. A small-cap and/or value "tilt" to one's portfolio was considered desirable in that it would earn, in expectation, a higher return, even after adjusting for risk. Today, only a minority of analysts would make that claim; they would propose, instead, that style and size categories of the market are (at least on average over time) fairly priced relative to one another, given their inherent risks. I argue briefly in this chapter that value may be a better long-term strategy than growth, but that is by no means a foregone conclusion.

Note the triple duty to which the concept of investment style is put:
1. a way of understanding the characteristics of individual stocks,
2. a way of describing a manager's approach to analyzing securities (thus, value managers would not necessarily buy "value stocks" but might look for attractive valuations anywhere), and
3. a way of building benchmarks—and thus of building index funds, conducting performance evaluation of managers, and managing active portfolios by using the benchmark weights as a starting point.

Because of the importance of size (capitalization) and of value versus growth in explaining stocks' performance, the styles generally identified in current practice are large-cap value, large-cap growth, small-cap value, and small-cap growth. A mid-cap category (divided into value and growth) is also often separated out. Finally, a "core" or "neutral" style (indicating that a stock or portfolio is neither value nor growth) is sometimes broken out.

This classification scheme permeates the investment world and has brought with it a proliferation of style-based funds and benchmarks. Although style as a concept is almost universally accepted, no definition or application of style is universally agreed upon; each index provider constructs style indexes differently. I will discuss how style investing developed and describe how indexes are constructed to measure this market segment.

Multiple Uses of the Style Concept

First, reflect on the three uses to which the value and growth concepts are put: to characterize individual stocks, to describe managers' investment styles, and to build indexes and benchmarks.

Value and Growth Stocks. The fact that stocks differ in their growth prospects, as well as in their valuation multiples, can be used to categorize them. Thus, Microsoft Corporation is typically regarded as a growth stock because it has experienced a 16.8 percent compound annual growth rate of earnings over the past five years; Whirlpool Corporation is a value stock because it has a price-to-earnings ratio (P/E) of 12.

Usually, however, a given stock is considered a value or growth stock because it is in a particular value or growth benchmark. Thus, a "value manager" with no specific views on the stock will hold it at its weight in the value benchmark. Once I've explored how style benchmarks are constructed, it will become clearer why you must be careful when calling a security a "value stock" or "growth stock" simply because it is in a given benchmark.

Value and Growth Managers. Some managers look for stocks selling at prices lower than the book value of their assets or lower even than net working capital; others look for high dividend yields or low P/Es. These managers are the classic "value managers," whose style predates the modern concept of style investing. Their strategy is where the value style got its name.

Classic "growth managers," in contrast, look for companies with the best long-term earnings growth prospects. They are less concerned about paying the lowest possible price.

Traditionally, most managers were neither value nor growth but used elements of both disciplines or ways of looking at the world. This description is still true for many managers today, but the need for managers to be classified as value or growth by consultants (in order to be hired by the consultants' clients) has caused managers to cluster into value and growth camps—mostly by sticking to stocks in their particular style benchmark.

Value and Growth Benchmarks. Finally, the concepts of value and growth are used to define benchmarks. This sense of "investment style" is the principal focus of this chapter. Typically, but not always, style benchmarks are designed so that a capitalization-weighted combination of them sums to the overall cap-weighted market. To achieve this result, most sets of benchmarks are constructed so that every stock is classified as either growth or value. Alternatively, the capitalization of a stock is split between the two categories; that is, the same stock appears in both the value and growth indexes, with (typically) the capitalization of the stock divided up so that an investor holding both indexes does not get a double weighting in the stock.

A different approach would be to have a third category—core or neutral— in which to put stocks that are neither growth nor value. Because the words "value" and "growth" connote extremes of valuation, the concept of a core or neutral category is intuitively appealing. Unfortunately, none of the index providers whose indexes are reviewed here has a separate core category for which it keeps track of returns and membership.[3] Consequently, many value or growth managers manage tracking error relative to a value or growth benchmark that contains core issues by buying these issues whether they are in keeping with the manager's philosophy and strategy or not.

Also note that the returns on value and growth benchmarks can be interpreted as *factors* (or *betas*), which are used to explain (statistically) the performance of stocks or of groups of stocks and to calculate the "pure alphas" and other performance statistics of managers (see Chapter 2).

---

[3]Morningstar, which constructs a suite of style indexes that are not reviewed here, does keep track of returns and constituent (stock) lists for the core category.

Some Caveats about Style Classification

Stocks classified into the value category are not necessarily underpriced; they may just appear to be. A low stock price may reflect the market's correct assessment of a company's current or future difficulties. A "good deal" can become a "better deal."

Investors should also be careful not to classify a stock as a growth issue simply because some investors or analysts have rosy expectations for the company. Graham and Zweig (2003) cautioned:

> If the definition of a growth stock is a company that will thrive in the future, then that's not a definition at all, but wishful thinking. It's like calling a sports team "the champions" before the season is over. This wishful thinking persists today; among mutual funds, "growth" portfolios describe their holdings as companies with "above-average growth potential" or "favorable prospects for earnings growth." A better definition might be companies whose net earnings per share have increased by 15 percent for at least five years running. Meeting this definition in the past does not ensure that a company will meet it in the future. (p. 581)

Growth and value benchmarks can have long stretches of exceptionally good or bad relative performance, Growth stocks outperformed value stocks at various times in the 1950s and 1960s; then, value regained the upper hand in the 1970s. More recently, the explosion of growth stocks in the 1990s, consisting mostly of Internet and technology stocks in the market bubble, has given way to a relative advantage for value stocks in recent years. The size of the divergence between returns of different styles is huge, which provides an opportunity to add alpha by changing your allocation to different equity styles. This return variability also shows why diversifying across growth and value segments of the market is important.

Although definitions of growth and value vary from investor to investor, depending on what the investor believes and is trying to achieve, index constructors do not have this luxury. An index must be rigorously and objectively constructed, relatively transparent as to methodology, and at the same time, intuitively appealing. The subjective nature of investment style makes it difficult, if not impossible, for a given index to meet all these criteria. As a result, style index construction methods differ considerably among index providers, so understanding these differences is vital.

Before discussing in detail the various style indexes and the methods used to construct them, I will review some of the research findings and theoretical advances that led to the development of style investing and style benchmarks.

The Evolution of Style Investing

Style investing and style benchmarks lie at the intersection of two threads of investment thinking: (1) traditional portfolio management and (2) quantitative academic research. As mentioned previously, value and growth approaches to security selection existed in the traditional investment management world long before any quantitative style factors were identified. As academics began to discover common statistical factors in stock returns other than the single market factor, they searched for real, or intuitive, factors with which to describe and identify the statistical factors. Value and growth were superbly preadapted to this use.

Traditional Approaches to Portfolio Management. Long before the terms "style," "value," and "growth" became commonplace, investors were already investing in line with these ideas. In 1934, Graham and Dodd argued in their book *Security Analysis* that investors should focus on company fundamentals and financial statement analysis and should buy the stocks of companies trading at less than their intrinsic value. This approach is the essence of value investing. Growth investing became a distinct strategy in the late 1950s and is associated with the work of Philip Fisher (e.g., 1958). It was embodied in the popularity in the early 1970s of the "Nifty Fifty," which were thriving companies (including Eastman Kodak Company, IBM Corporation, and McDonald's Corporation) that steadily rose in price despite lofty valuations. Investors were bidding up the prices in the expectation that earnings would grow even more in the future.

Quantitative Academic Research. The development of the CAPM in the 1960s, as described in Chapter 4, and its popularity in the following decade set researchers to the task of proving it wrong. One way to cast doubt on a theory is to find a persistent "anomaly" or set of facts that is unexplained by the theory. Academic researchers set out to find anomalies and ended up using some of them to develop factor models, define styles, and create style benchmarks.

■ *The size (capitalization) effect.* With hundreds of assistant professors looking to make their mark, someone was sure to find something anomalous in the market, but few were expecting anything as dramatic as the finding by Rolf Banz in 1979 that small-cap stocks—stocks with the smaller equity capitalizations (as measured by price times number of shares outstanding)—had a much higher average return than large-cap stocks (see Banz 1981).[4] Gavin Hall of Delaware International Advisers recalled:

> The Banz research covered the years 1936–1975 and, on average, the very smallest stocks on the NYSE (bottom 50) outperformed the very largest (top 50) by just over 100 basis points per month.[5]

---

[4]More detail on the small-cap effect and on the history surrounding its discovery can be found in Clothier, Waring, and Siegel (1998).

[5]"Investing in International Small Company Stocks," Institute for Fiduciary Education website: www.ifecorp.com/Papers-PDFs/Hall701.pdf.

Reinganum (1981) independently discovered the same effect.

Even if you do not compare only the very smallest with the very largest stocks, the return difference discovered by Banz and Reinganum was huge when compounded over long time periods—and it was not explained by beta.[6] (If small-cap stocks had higher betas—high enough to explain the higher returns—that fact would take away the mystery or "anomaly" with respect to the CAPM.)

Several explanations for the small-cap effect are possible. First, the market might not be efficient; small-cap stocks might have been underpriced, thus yielding higher returns over the period that Banz and Reinganum studied. Second, small size might be a proxy for some sort of risk that is being priced by the market but that is not measured by beta; if so, then the small-cap effect is the delivery of a risk premium. The second explanation, in other words, says that small size is a risk factor. This risk-factor explanation for the size effect has been more widely accepted since Fama and French clearly advocated it in 1992.

■   *The valuation effect.* At roughly the same time as the work of Banz and Reinganum, Basu (1977, 1983) independently discovered that low-P/E stocks have higher returns than high-P/E stocks (again, after adjustment for beta).[7] Using price-to-book-value (P/B) produces much the same result (see Rosenberg, Reid, and Lanstein 1985). Again, either the market is inefficient or P/E is serving as a proxy for some sort of risk not captured by a stock's beta.

Although the reaction of some practitioners to this research was, "Ho hum; underpriced stocks beat overpriced stocks. We knew that," the surprise registered by academic researchers in response to the discovery of the value and size effects is hard to overstate. More than a decade of efficient market and CAPM orthodoxy had convinced most that the cap-weighted market portfolio could not be beaten, at least not with a simple, easy-to-follow decision rule. Yet, here was a collection of properly trained, careful researchers, wielding seemingly accurate data, who claimed that not one but two very profitable such rules existed! These findings created a "crisis" in CAPM thinking from which the theory has never fully recovered. Almost no one today believes that the market is completely efficient or that the CAPM precisely describes the relationship between risk and expected return.

Now that the barn door was open, researchers rushed to discover new factors—new systematic ways to beat the market without taking any added risk

---

[6]Some authors have argued that the small-cap effect is smaller, or disappears, if one calculates beta in a way that takes account of infrequent trading and other circumstances peculiar to small-cap stocks. The most recent entry in a large body of literature is Ibbotson, Kaplan, and Peterson (1997).

[7]Ball (1978) and others made similar discoveries around the same time.

(as measured by beta). Most of the factors that were subsequently discovered, however, turned out to be proxies for valuation (or, occasionally, size).

One new factor that looked promising—and that was unrelated to any previously discovered factor—was *momentum* (see Jegadeesh 1990). This discovery was another surprise for efficient market theorists. (I do not cover momentum in this monograph.)

From Factors to Styles. The investment management consulting firms seized on the discovery of the size and valuation effects pretty quickly and began advising clients to achieve maximum diversification by, at first, adding small-cap funds and, later, adding value- and growth-focused funds to their asset mixes. Consultants had already observed that managers' approaches to making investment choices clustered into value and growth categories, and the factors discovered by academics mapped nicely in these categories.

Who was the first to label factor exposures as "styles" is not clear, but by 1988, when Sharpe published his methodology for identifying the factor exposures of a portfolio through regression analysis, the term he used—"returns-based style analysis"—was perfectly well understood by the profession. A more formal write-up by Sharpe in 1992 solidified the use of style analysis in general and of large-cap, small-cap, growth, and value as the choices.

The public understanding of investment styles was greatly aided by Morningstar's decision in the early 1990s to classify mutual funds into the now-familiar three-by-three system of style boxes and to develop the Morningstar style-box "icon," which indicates the style of a given fund. In 1996, Morningstar changed its classification system from a traditional one ("growth," "growth and income," "equity income," and so forth) to one based on the modern conception of styles. As a result of these decisions, mutual funds are now typically named and marketed in ways that explicitly refer to their investment styles.

▪ *Sharpe and returns-based style analysis.* The work of Basu, Banz, Rosenberg, and others indicated how to rank stocks by size and valuation and, as a result, provided a strong suggestion for how to map stocks into styles. Determining the style of an actively managed portfolio with changing portfolio contents is harder, however, than determining the style of a stock. For this purpose, Sharpe proposed using a type of regression to analyze the historical returns of a portfolio to measure the portfolio's exposures to, say, four well-defined style benchmarks. The return history of the portfolio, he argued, leaves "tracks in the sand" that indicate what style or mix of styles was followed.

One of Sharpe's principal innovations was to emphasize that virtually all portfolios—all portfolios except style index funds—represent a mix of styles. In other words, style is scalar; it is a continuum. As an example, a portfolio that is generally considered to be large-cap growth could be identified as 70 percent large-cap growth, 20 percent large-cap value, 5 percent small-cap growth, and 5 percent small-cap value. These weights may be viewed as the "style betas" of the portfolio, that is, the betas resulting from the regression of the portfolio's returns on those of the style factors. They are the extent to which the portfolio's returns are influenced, or explained, by the return on each of the style benchmarks.

In addition, Sharpe's work enabled a plan sponsor to disentangle a manager's style bets—intended or unintended—from the pure alpha added by the manager. This technology allows sponsors to manage the various risks of the portfolio and to identify managers who actually add alpha relative to a properly style-adjusted benchmark (see Chapter 2 and also Waring and Siegel 2003).

To conduct returns-based style analysis, you need to have well-constructed benchmarks. While other researchers were focusing on P/E, Sharpe decided to focus on P/B as the valuation measure for classifying stocks into styles. Sharpe's choice of P/B has influenced the construction of style benchmarks to this day, and Sharpe's work was one of the motivations for the consulting industry to develop such benchmarks.

An example of Sharpe's returns-based style analysis is in **Figure 8.1**. The example shows that Fidelity's Magellan Fund was initially exposed in a large degree to small-cap growth but that large-cap value increased in the mid-1990s. Over the whole period, large-cap growth was expanding as an influence on the fund, and by April 2000, it explained most of the fund's return.[8]

■ *Fama and French's three-factor model.* Fama and French (1992, 1993) extended the investigation of the size- and valuation-related anomalies that had been identified more than a decade earlier by backdating the analysis to 1926. Their results, updated to 2003, for large-cap value and growth portfolios are in **Figure 8.2**. Value beat growth by a large margin over this span, but as **Table 8.1** shows, when the data are adjusted for risk by calculation of the Sharpe ratio, the margin is not nearly as large as it looks.

Note from Table 8.1 that the Fama–French large-cap value index was riskier, statistically, than the growth index. This outcome is somewhat surprising, in that value stocks seem safer because of their lower multiples and because value indexes have been less volatile in the experience of investors living today. In the Great Depression of the 1930s, however, the value index fell twice as far as the growth index (in the logarithmic sense; the 90 percent decline in value left the investor with half as much money as the 80 percent decline in growth). This event lends support to Fama and French's contention that the value effect is the delivery of a risk premium, not evidence of market inefficiency.

---

[8]The analysis depicted in Figure 8.1 is based on a rolling 60-month data window; that is, the style exposure shown for each month represents the average style exposure over the five years ending in that month.

**Figure 8.1. Returns-Based Style Analysis: Fidelity Magellan Fund,
June 1982–April 2000**

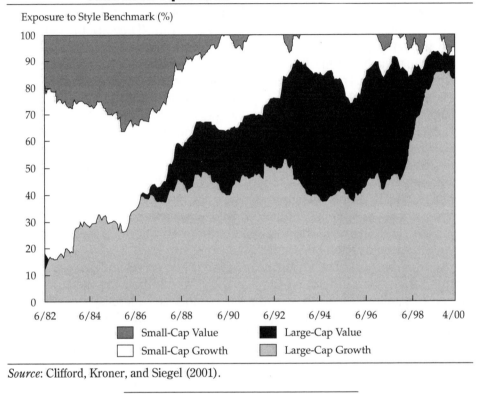

Source: Clifford, Kroner, and Siegel (2001).

Surprisingly, over the period examined by Fama and French, which eventually extended back to 1924, the size and valuation effects were so powerful that these effects eliminated beta as an explanatory variable for stock returns. The work of Fama and French was interpreted as meaning "beta is dead." Over certain periods, however, beta has been a useful explanatory variable (and the logic of the CAPM, which states that beta is the only explanatory variable, is too compelling to jettison entirely).[9] As a result, Fama

---

[9]Beta worked well during the period leading up to the time, in the early 1960s, when Sharpe discovered it, but in the period from 1963 to 1990, the relationship between beta and stock returns was not clear. Instead, Fama and French found that size and book-to-price ratio (B/P, the inverse of P/B) had the greatest power to explain returns. Responding to criticism, they found, by looking at ever longer periods, that the results still held: Size and valuation swamped the effect of beta for 1924–1990. Fama and French showed that B/P is more effective than size at explaining returns and, in fact, when combined with size, renders the other factors (E/P and leverage) redundant.

Figure 8.2. Cumulative Returns on Fama–French Value and Growth Portfolios, July 1926–January 2003

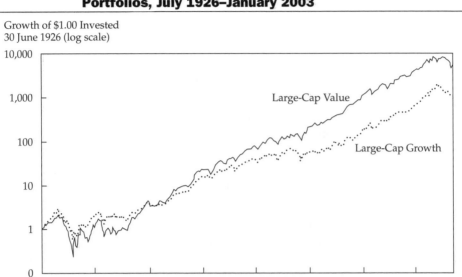

Source: Kenneth R. French's website, mba.tuck.dartmouth.edu/pages/faculty/ken.french/, which updates work in Fama and French (1992).

Table 8.1. Summary Statistics of Returns on Fama–French Large-Cap Value and Growth Portfolios, July 1927–January 2003

Statistic	Large-Cap Value	Large-Cap Growth
Compound annual return (%)	11.71	9.48
Arithmetic mean return (%)	14.30	10.92
Annualized standard deviation (%)	25.89	19.08
Sharpe ratio[a]	0.408	0.377

[a]Calculated in excess of U.S. Treasury bill return.

Source: Calculated by the author using data from French (see note to Figure 8.2).

and French adopted a three-factor approach to explaining and predicting the returns on a given stock:

$$r_i = r_f + \beta_1 (r_m - r_f) + \beta_2 (SMB) + \beta_3 (HML) + \tilde{\varepsilon},$$

where

r_i	= return on stock or portfolio i
r_f	= riskless rate of return
r_m	= return on the cap-weighted market index
SMB	= "small minus big"; the return on a small-cap portfolio minus the return on a large-cap portfolio
HML	= "high minus low"; return on a high-B/P (i.e., value) portfolio minus the return on a low-B/P (i.e., growth) portfolio
β_1, β_2, and β_3	= betas (or loading factors) on, respectively, the market factor, SMB, and HML
$\tilde{\varepsilon}$	= random error term with an expected value of zero

This model can be understood as expectational (i.e., as with the CAPM, you put in the expected value for each right-hand-side variable to arrive at the expected return on stock or portfolio i) or as backward looking (i.e., as with the market model, you run a regression to see what factor exposures best explain the return on stock or portfolio i). Using this model, you can express any stock or portfolio as a mixture of exposures to three factors—beta, size, and valuation.

Although the functional form of the Fama–French model is quite different from that of Sharpe's approach, the content is similar. Both methods strongly validate style as a way of understanding investment performance, and both provide a way to use returns (not holdings) to identify the style of a stock or portfolio. Like Sharpe, Fama and French used book value, not earnings or other variables, to capture the fundamental value of the firm. Although book value is not completely satisfying from an economic point of view, it is less volatile than earnings and provides strong style differentiation (that is, value and growth indexes formed using P/B have very different returns).

■ *An evaluation of Fama–French.* Is the value effect really the delivery of a risk premium, implying that all styles are priced fairly? The idea that the value premium is a risk premium seems a little *ad hoc* to me. I suspect that if growth stocks had beaten value stocks historically, or large cap had beaten small cap, someone would have proposed a theory saying that a high growth rate (or large size) is a source of special risk for which investors demand, and in the long run receive, a higher return. Positing a "risk premium" to explain whatever factor delivers a superior return smacks of an attempt to preserve efficient market theory in the face of strong evidence against it.

If, instead, the market is inefficient and the value premium is the manifestation of this inefficiency, then value investing is a better strategy than growth investing. But although the market is probably inefficient, simply overweighting value stocks as a way to consistently earn a superior risk-adjusted return is too easy. Simple rule-based systems for beating the market tend to work only until they're discovered. High-beta stocks beat low-beta stocks until William Sharpe discovered beta in 1964; small-cap stocks beat large-cap ones until Banz and Reinganum discovered the size effect in 1979; and the value premium may yet be subject to the same fate.

Investors are powerfully motivated to exploit and eliminate, not just discover and write papers about, profitable market anomalies. For this reason, although underpaying for assets is a better idea than overpaying, value investing as it is currently defined may not be a winner in the indefinite future. Value investing of some kind will probably be a winner, but value may not be defined as low P/E or low P/B. There has been plenty of time (and plenty of capital at work) to arbitrage away the value–growth disparity as defined by these widely followed factors. The winning combination of stocks in the future is likely to be described by a factor or mix of factors that hasn't been discovered yet.

Another way of expressing this thought is to say that prudent investors, no matter what their stated styles, must do the homework of assessing the fundamental value of a stock and comparing that value with the stock's price. Such a discipline is currently associated more with value investing than with growth investing, but it should pervade all security analysis. If you wait long enough, market prices *always* tend toward fundamental value.

■ *Holdings-based vs. returns-based style analysis.* An alternative method of identifying the style of a portfolio is called "holdings-based style analysis" because it uses the characteristics of the securities in a portfolio at a given time as the basis for estimating the manager's likely future style exposures. Returns-based and holdings-based style analyses have different advantages and disadvantages.[10] Holdings-based analysis is up-to-date as of the time of the analysis, whereas returns-based analysis relies on a moving data window and thus incorporates results from a style that the manager may no longer be following. Holdings-based analysis can also become out-of-date quickly, however, because managers can change holdings at any time.

The main problem with holdings-based style analysis is that it requires up-to-date, security-level data and risk-factor exposure estimates for each security for each fund that is being analyzed. Return data are much easier to

---

[10]The case for holdings-based style analysis is made by Buetow, Johnson, and Runkle (2000). A number of other authors have made similar arguments.

obtain. Moreover, if you are trying to estimate the historical "pure alpha" described in Chapter 2 (which I argued is the only historical return measure relevant for forecasting a manager's future alpha), you would need data on the holdings *across* time, which are just about impossible to get. Returns-based style analysis, while possibly less precise, has much less formidable data requirements and inherently incorporates changes in the manager's style over the period for which the alpha is being calculated.

Commercial Style Indexes. After factors that map into styles had been identified, the remaining step was to build style benchmarks. Like other benchmarks, style benchmarks (or indexes) are paper portfolios representing the factors or styles that have constituent lists updated in real time and daily return calculation so that indexers can see what securities to buy and active managers can have a benchmark against which to run a portfolio.

The natural providers of these style indexes were the companies that were already providing other types of indexes. In the mid-1980s, Wilshire Associates and the Frank Russell Company became the first companies to build style indexes. Standard & Poor's (originally in collaboration with Sharpe and with Barra) and Dow Jones and Company also constructed style indexes of the U.S. equity market.[11] In the next section, I discuss the characteristics of these suites of style indexes and assess the trade-offs involved in constructing them.

Index Construction and Trade-Offs

Style and size indexes of U.S. equities differ from one another much more than do the unstylized, broad-cap indexes discussed in Chapter 1. As a result, the investor must understand the methods used to construct the various style indexes in order to decide which index to use and to know how to use it. In the next discussions, I describe in detail how four of the leading suites of U.S. equity style indexes are constructed and comment on the merits and demerits of each. Then, I discuss the special trade-offs involved in style index construction. Particular attention should be paid to the factors used to classify stocks into styles; some style indexes use one factor (e.g., P/B)—others use multiple factors.

Size Indexes. This discussion of style index construction begins with size because size indexes are built first; index constructors do not assign growth or value designations to stocks at the broad market level. They first break up the broad market into size-specific indexes and then subdivide the

---

[11]All of these indexes are described in detail later. Additional providers of style indexes for the U.S. equity market, including Morgan Stanley Capital International and Morningstar, are not covered here.

size indexes into style subindexes. This approach is sensible because style factors interact with the size factor. For example, large-cap stocks tend to have higher P/Bs. If style were determined at the broad market level, growth indexes would be biased toward large-cap stocks and value indexes would be even more biased than they are toward small-cap stocks.

Although determining the capitalization of a stock is relatively straightforward (the only controversial aspect being float adjustment), the various index constructors differ on how to divide stocks into large-, mid-, and small-cap categories. **Exhibit 8.1** outlines the methodology for each major suite of indexes. (Capitalization statistics and fundamental characteristics for the size indexes and the style indexes are provided later in this chapter.)

Exhibit 8.1. Size Index Inclusion Criteria

Provider	Large	Mid Cap	Small Cap
S&P	Committee selection of 500 industry-leading companies	Committee selection of 400 companies	Committee selection of 600 companies
Russell	Top 200 companies by market cap at reconstitution date	Next 800 companies (ranked 201 to 1,000 by market cap)	Next 2,000 companies (ranked 1,001 to 3,000 by market cap)
Dow Jones	Top 70 percent of float-adjusted market cap	Next 20 percent of float-adjusted cap (70–90%)	Next 5 percent (90–95%)
Wilshire Style	Top 750 companies by market cap	500 companies ranked 501 to 1,000; combination of large cap and small cap	Next 1,750 after large cap (ranked 751 to 2,500)

Size indexes also differ in the timing of their reconstitutions, rules for rebalancing because of changing numbers of shares and other corporate actions, rules for deleting stocks and (potentially) replacing them, and many other variables. Before moving on to style indexes, I will briefly touch on the differences between the principal suites of size indexes.

■ *Standard & Poor's.* The S&P 500 Index was originally created as a broad-cap index; only more recently has the S&P 500 been viewed as a large-cap index and the S&P 400 (mid-cap) and S&P 600 (small cap) been added. The S&P indexes are not governed by strict market-cap guidelines and include companies regarded by the S&P index committee as "industry leaders" or "representative companies" regardless of their market cap. For all indexes constructed by Standard & Poor's, inclusion and removal decisions are made by the index committee rather than by formulaic decision rules.

■ *Frank Russell Company.* The Frank Russell Company developed its Top 200 and mid-cap indexes as subsets of the Russell 1000. The company refers to the Russell 1000 as "representing large-cap stocks" and uses the trademark "Top 200" to differentiate this specialized index from the Russell 1000, which I am treating as a large- and mid-cap index.

■ *Dow Jones.* Unlike the other index constructors, Dow Jones has implemented buffer rules to reduce turnover within the capitalization indexes. For example, a large-cap company that ranks in the top 75 percent of the capitalization of the market will not be deleted from the large-cap index even though it needs to rank in the top 70 percent to be included in the first place. Similar buffer rules apply to the other capitalization strata.[12]

■ *Wilshire Style.* Wilshire Associates constructs two suites of indexes, called "style" and "target" indexes. The style indexes are calculated "to evaluate the performance of active managers," and the target indexes represent more concentrated portfolios intended to be held as style index funds. Throughout this chapter, I refer only to the style indexes and use the phrase "Wilshire Style" consistently to clarify that point. The mid-cap Wilshire Style index is not a separate segment of the overall market but an overlay, consisting of the bottom 250 stocks in the large-cap Wilshire Style index plus the top 250 stocks in the small-cap Wilshire Style index.

Creating the Style Indexes. All of the index constructors draw on the research findings discussed earlier in this chapter, but the four major constructors differ in the way they define their growth and value indexes. The only common threads are that they assign style at the capitalization level and that they use P/Bs as at least part of the input. The indexes differ as to what factors besides P/B, if any, to use and how the factors are used to assign stocks to one category or another. **Exhibit 8.2** summarizes their construction rules. The most important differences between the suites of style indexes are as follows.

■ *Standard & Poor's.* For each capitalization index, S&P uses the rank of the stocks by P/B to split the total cap of that stratum so that 50 percent is in the value index and 50 percent is in the growth index. In other words, each company is classified as "all growth" or "all value" on the basis of its P/B as of the reconstitution day. Because growth companies tend to be larger than value companies, the growth index has fewer stocks than the value index.

■ *Frank Russell Company.* The factors used by Russell are P/B and the I/B/E/S consensus long-term growth average (that is, one accounting ratio and one projection or estimate).[13] The total capitalization of the market is split

---

[12]For more detail, see Pope, Rakvin, and Platt (2003).

[13]I/B/E/S data are now part of the First Call database maintained by Thomson Financial.

Exhibit 8.2. Style Index Construction Rules

Provider	Exclusive or Split Classification[a]	Value + Growth Indexes Sum to Market	Transparency of Factor Model	Factors
S&P	Exclusive	Yes	Transparent—ranking by one variable	P/B
Russell	Split	Yes	Proprietary (not transparent)	P/B I/B/E/S long-term growth estimate
Dow Jones	Exclusive	No	Proprietary (not transparent)	P/B Projected P/E Projected EPS growth Trailing P/E Trailing EPS growth Dividend yield
Wilshire Style	Exclusive	No	Partly transparent	P/B Projected P/E

[a]Exclusive: 100 percent of the capitalization of each stock is assigned to a single style (value, growth, or in some cases, core). Split: The cap of a stock may be split between value and growth.

50–50, but Russell uses an algorithm to classify each stock into one of three categories—all value, all growth, or split between the two. The result is that 70 percent of stocks are 100 percent growth or value and 30 percent are split. The splits are typically uneven (for example, a stock might be, depending on its P/B and estimated growth rate, 25 percent value and 75 percent growth). Russell does not publish the style algorithm, which was created in 1993.

Russell assigns style at the Russell 1000 level and breaks this index up into large cap and mid cap. The result, because large-cap stocks naturally trade at a higher P/B, is that 55 percent of the Russell Top 200 is classified as growth whereas only 40 percent of the Russell Midcap is classified this way.

■ *Dow Jones.* Dow Jones uses six factors—P/B, projected and trailing P/E, projected and trailing earnings per share (EPS) growth, and dividend yield. Thus, Dow Jones combines a wide variety of historical and projected data. Like Russell, Dow Jones has a proprietary statistical process to translate the raw data into growth–value splits. Each stock is classified as 100 percent growth, 100 percent value, or neutral. Unlike the other index providers, Dow Jones does not split the total capitalization of the market evenly between growth and value.

■ *Wilshire Style.* For each capitalization index, Wilshire classifies stocks into styles by P/B and projected P/E, with P/B given three times the weight of P/E. The total capitalization of the market is split 50–50, and stocks are classified as either 100 percent growth or 100 percent value.

Capitalization statistics of the principal style indexes are in **Table 8.2**. The relationship between style and size index construction methods, on the one hand, and the performance of those indexes, on the other hand, could and should be a book in itself and is not covered here. Suffice it to say that the performance differences between different equity indexes purporting to measure the same style or size category tend to be large, whereas the performance differences between most other types of indexes are small.

Trade-Offs in Style Index Construction. Because it is important to understand the fine points of style index construction before selecting and using a suite of indexes, this section provides a detailed discussion of the trade-offs in constructing style indexes.

■ *How many style factors? Simplicity vs. explanatory power.* P/B (or its inverse, B/P) is the one factor that is used, at least in part, by all of the index constructors. Its use is supported by the work of Sharpe (1988, 1992) and Fama and French (1993). Standard & Poor's uses only the P/B to classify stocks. The other index providers use other factors in addition to P/B and use them in a variety of ways.

A small number of style factors achieves the virtues of simplicity and transparency. The only set of indexes constructed by sorting stocks on the basis of one variable is that created by S&P (which does, however, apply judgment in building the size indexes out of which the style subindexes are carved). Any combination of variables introduces a degree of opaqueness. Price, book value, and earnings are public information, so investors and managers can predict with considerable accuracy the results of a sorting of stocks by *either* P/B or P/E. When the P/B and P/E factors are combined, however, as in the Wilshire indexes, the investor would have to know the precise algorithm to correctly predict the results of the index reconstitution (it is not enough to know that P/B has three times the weight of P/E).

All other things being equal, a predictable and transparent style classification system reduces transaction costs. The major reason is that brokers and hedge funds create liquidity in anticipation of style index reconstitutions by buying stocks they think they can sell to index funds and benchmark-sensitive active funds and by shorting stocks they think they can buy from these funds. The ability of brokers and hedge funds to create liquidity in this way—and, correspondingly, the ability of indexers and index-sensitive active managers to keep their transaction costs under control—depends on the simplicity and transparency of the style classification system.

Table 8.2. Capitalization Statistics of Principal U.S. Equity Size and Style Indexes, 31 December 2002

($ in thousands)

Style/Statistic	S&P	Russell[b]	Dow Jones Total Market	Wilshire Style
Large cap				
Number of stocks	500	198	215	743
Market cap of total index ($)	8,107,546,624	6,349,761,024	6,481,344,000	8,850,116,608
Largest-stock cap ($)	276,411,456	241,984,720	242,269,616	276,411,456
Smallest-stock cap ($)	279,286	3,246,933	2,199,620	193,899
Weighted-average market cap ($)	76,711,000	89,776,000	88,190,000	71,479,000
Historical inception date	January 1926[a]	January 1979	December 1991	January 1978
Mid cap				
Number of stocks	400	793	504	497
Market cap of total index ($)	702,908,736	2,040,461,696	1,690,023,168	819,479,872
Largest-stock cap ($)	7,292,344	10,345,811	10,213,473	11,124,001
Smallest-stock cap ($)	132,473	120,150	265,080	144,647
Weighted-average market cap ($)	2,513,000	4,562,000	4,933,000	1,997,000
Historical inception date	February 1981[c]	January 1979	December 1991	January 1978
Small cap				
Number of stocks	600	1,964	859	1,729
Market cap of total index ($)	325,187,456	601,010,432	654,667,392	952,756,416
Largest-stock cap ($)	2,685,695	1,769,077	3,030,933	5,032,104
Smallest-stock cap ($)	39,165	3,790	26,455	13,494
Weighted-average market cap ($)	832,000	628,000	1,246,000	878,000
Historical inception date	March 1984[c]	January 1979	December 1991	January 1978
Large-cap value				
Number of stocks	352	143	113	496
Market cap of total index ($)	4,023,928,320	2,952,911,872	3,494,580,736	4,327,615,488
Largest-stock cap ($)	235,107,696	236,963,808	236,104,992	180,745,248
Smallest-stock cap ($)	279,286	673,222	4,070,547	193,899
Weighted-average market cap ($)	51,645,000	71,860,000	76,045,000	849,000
Historical inception date	January 1975	January 1986	June 1997	January 1978
Mid-cap value				
Number of stocks	241	607	204	243
Market cap of total index ($)	356,468,288	1,187,835,264	752,874,432	393,134,336
Largest-stock cap ($)	4,895,093	10,222,605	10,213,473	3,799,880
Smallest-stock cap ($)	132,473	15,953	318,053	438,214
Weighted-average market cap ($)	2,079,000	4,362,000	4,988,000	1,850,000
Historical inception date	June 1991[c]	January 1986	June 1997	January 1978

Table 8.2. Capitalization Statistics of Principal U.S. Equity Size and Style Indexes, 31 December 2002 (continued)

($ in thousands)

Style/Statistic	S&P	Russell[b]	Dow Jones Total Market	Wilshire Style
Small-cap value				
Number of stocks	390	1,325	295	890
Market cap of total index ($)	163,973,888	307,850,816	251,129,552	459,626,496
Largest-stock cap ($)	1,602,840	1,358,273	2,265,744	5,032,104
Smallest-stock cap ($)	39,165	2,031	26,455	13,494
Weighted-average market cap ($)	613,000	609,000	1,263,000	874,000[d]
Historical inception date	January 1994[c]	January 1979	June 1997	January 1978
Large-cap growth				
Number of stocks	500	198	215	743
Market cap of total index ($)	8,107,546,624	6,349,761,024	6,481,344,000	8,850,116,608
Largest-stock cap ($)	276,411,456	241,984,720	242,269,616	276,411,456
Smallest-stock cap ($)	279,286	3,246,933	2,199,620	193,899
Weighted-average market cap ($)	76,711,000	89,776,000	88,190,000	71,479,000
Historical inception date	January 1975	January 1986	June 1997	January 1978
Mid-cap growth				
Number of stocks	159	454	189	254
Market cap of total index ($)	346,440,672	852,627,008	600,589,504	426,346,080
Largest-stock cap ($)	7,292,344	10,345,811	9,966,566	11,124,001
Smallest-stock cap ($)	334,565	13,402	347,146	144,647
Weighted-average market cap ($)	2,959,000	4,840,000	4,983,000	2,132,000
Historical inception date	June 1991[c]	January 1986	June 1997	January 1978
Small-cap growth				
Number of stocks	210	1,278	286	839
Market cap of total index ($)	161,213,376	293,159,456	192,439,200	493,131,040
Largest-stock cap ($)	2,685,695	1,530,137	3,030,933	3,900,638
Smallest-stock cap ($)	81,995	1,150	45,269	16,684
Weighted-average market cap ($)	1,055,000	648,000	1,202,000	99,362,000
Historical inception date	January 1994[c]	January 1979	June 1997	January 1978

[a]The S&P 500 data start March 1957 and have been linked by Ibbotson Associates (2003) with a predecessor index, the S&P 90, to form a continuous series from 1926 to the present.
[b]The Russell large-cap index described here is the Top 200. The Russell 1000 (Top 200 plus mid-cap 800) is also sometimes referred to as a large-cap index.
[c]Survival biases are known to affect the historically reconstructed S&P mid-cap and small-cap indexes, including style indexes.
[d]Data as of 30 June 2003.

Source: Pope, Rakvin, and Platt (2003).

On the one hand, because book value is less volatile than earnings, an index constructed by using only book value and price produces more stable portfolios and thus lower transaction costs upon reconstitution. Moreover, proponents of P/B as the sole factor argue that the price-to-book ratio captures all the relevant information contained in the other factors. If it does, then using additional factors is simply redundant, in addition to subtracting from transparency. Furthermore, projected data (such as expected earnings growth) are subject to interpretation and revision, in contrast to accounting data, which are relatively fixed once the numbers are released. The problems with expected earnings growth are especially severe for small-cap stocks that are covered by few analysts.

On the other hand, it is not clear how book value could be so powerful in explaining the cross-section of stock returns that it wipes out the effect of P/E, growth expectations, and other potential factors. Book value is mostly a historical accident. It is the accounting profession's estimate of the company's value; it reflects what the company paid for its assets, except intangible assets, such as goodwill developed internally, but it includes the goodwill of subsidiary companies acquired by purchase. This "cost basis" is then adjusted downward by depreciation and amortization in a highly stylized and rigid attempt to reflect the economic depreciation that actually befalls (most) assets. Off-balance-sheet items are ignored. Finally, the result is augmented by retained earnings. With book value reflecting such a mélange, it is a wonder it has any explanatory power at all for differentiating value from growth stocks—but it does.

Logically, then, additional factors should provide additional information. Because, for example, "growth" might not be the exact opposite of "value," investors might be especially interested in the incremental explanatory power of factors that have nothing to do with valuation but, instead, reflect historical growth and/or expectations for future growth.

A multifactor approach to equity style classification was pioneered by Rosenberg, Reid, and Lanstein (1985). Although this topic has not attracted much subsequent attention from academics, who have mostly focused on P/B as the single style metric, the various index providers who use multifactor methods have done extensive research to support these methods.

Some analysts claim, in support of a multifactor approach, that P/B does not properly describe certain sectors. For example, companies in the technology sector may have understated book values because of intangible assets that are not capitalized. The result is that technology companies have elevated P/Bs, which classifies most of them as growth whether they should be or not. Including other factors could help overcome problems with P/Bs in describing style.

■ *Completeness vs. style purity.* One generally desirable trait of a set of style indexes is that they sum to the overall broad market index. When they do, investors can build a complete asset-allocation strategy—one that does not exclude important components of the market—by combining various style indexes.

The disadvantage of value and growth indexes that sum to the market is that such indexes are not "style pure." The value index includes many stocks (often with large weights) that are actually style neutral or somewhat "growthy." Similarly, the growth index includes stocks that could be construed as neutral or value stocks. By excluding core or neutral stocks, an index constructor provides a better representation of the universes from which style-focused active managers typically select their stocks. Style-pure indexes also provide better return differentiation for the purpose of measuring historical returns and understanding the behavior of the value and growth styles.

The S&P and Russell style indexes do sum to the market portfolio. This attribute is called "completeness." Subindexes that sum to a broader index are also sometimes called a "spanning set."

The Dow Jones value and growth indexes are not a spanning set because they exclude core or neutral stocks; they are thus more style pure than S&P and Russell style indexes. Dow Jones' neutral classification is not investable because performance and constituent (stock) weights are not calculated for this category. Furthermore, Dow Jones requires that each company have data for at least one projected factor and at least three historical factors (out of the six total factors). If a company fails to meet this requirement, it is removed from the universe entirely. This rule is likely to exclude most initial public offerings. Even if you could purchase the neutral index, the broad market index could not be re-created using Dow Jones style indexes since the IPOs would be missing.

The Wilshire Style value and growth indexes do sum to the size stratum of the market from which they are drawn. The mid-cap index, however, is an overlay consisting of some stocks from the small-cap index and some from the large-cap index. Thus, an investor would not be able to exclude mid-cap stocks from an otherwise broad market strategy by using Wilshire Style indexes. An investor could include mid-caps (without double weighting them), however, simply by buying the large- and small-cap indexes and avoiding the mid-cap overlay.

Morningstar, the leading provider of mutual fund data and ratings to retail investors, has a style classification system in which core is a separate style and the returns and index contents are tracked (see Phillips and Kaplan 2003). Morningstar's system, however, has not yet attracted a meaningful institutional following.

■ *Exclusive vs. split classification.* The question of whether to split a stock's capitalization between value and growth indexes is separate from the completeness or spanning question. Most sets of indexes (S&P, Dow Jones, and Wilshire Style) have a requirement that each stock be classified as 100 percent value or 100 percent growth (or, in the case of Wilshire Style, 100 percent neutral). Alternatively, an index provider could split the capitalization of a stock between growth and value so that the name appears in both the value and growth indexes, as Russell does.

As market prices and fundamental variables change, stocks move between the value and growth categories. Being able to split a stock reflects the fact that many stocks are in transition between the categories, and it reduces turnover, which is costly to investors. (Splitting reduces turnover because stocks close to the value–growth boundary do not have 100 percent of their capitalization jump back and forth from one category to another.) It also expands the selection universe for managers who choose from among the stocks in their style benchmark.

Style indexes created by splitting stocks may be confusing at first, however, because many of the same companies appear in both value and growth indexes. The index constructors who use buffer rules argue that reduction in turnover may be accomplished as effectively by using these rules as by splitting the capitalization of stocks between two different style indexes.

■ *Reconstitution/rebalancing frequency vs. turnover.* As noted in Chapter 1, reconstitution and rebalancing are sources of turnover, which, in turn, imposes transaction costs on investors. Turnover-related costs in style indexes are particularly sensitive to reconstitution frequency because a company can migrate back and forth between styles. The capitalization splits and buffer rules that are used by some index constructors mitigate this problem.

I now review the reconstitution and rebalancing practices of each major provider. Because the basic (not style) S&P indexes contain a fixed number of stocks and membership is decided by committee, these indexes are essentially reconstituted on an *ad hoc* basis. Any company deleted because of a corporate action (e.g., merger) is replaced by another company selected by the index committee. Additionally, Standard & Poor's may remove companies at the committee's discretion. Standard & Poor's also rebalances its indexes each quarter because of changes in the constituent companies' numbers of shares outstanding. The S&P style indexes are reconstituted semiannually.

The Frank Russell Company reconstitutes its indexes annually and does not replace companies between reconstitutions, so deletions resulting from corporate actions do not result in additional membership changes. Instead, the number of companies in the index shrinks until the next reconstitution date. Russell rebalances the index monthly to reflect changes in the number of shares.

The bulk of Russell's reconstitution of its capitalization, style, and overall indexes is done at the end of each June. Capitalization and style classifications occur only during this time and do not change during the following year.

The predictability and magnitude of the Russell reconstitution attracts a great deal of speculation from index funds and benchmark-sensitive managers attempting to trade ahead of the reconstitution and from brokers and hedge funds taking the other side of the trade. These attempts to profit from the anticipated reconstitution often result in temporary price distortions (see "Russell Mania" in Chapter 7).

Like Russell, Dow Jones adds companies only during the scheduled quarterly reconstitutions of its size and style indexes. Rebalancing because of changes in shares outstanding for index constituents is also done quarterly. The only adjustments made between reconstitutions are those resulting from corporate actions, which causes the number of stocks in the Dow Jones indexes to shrink because deleted companies are not replaced until the next reconstitution.

Wilshire updates its overall universe monthly. The number of shares outstanding for each company is updated, and IPOs are added to the index. The capitalization and style indexes, however, are reconstituted only once a year.

Conclusion

U.S. equity style indexes developed out of the traditional methods that managers historically used to identify desirable stocks. These methods coalesced into "styles" as academic researchers sought, and found, common factors in the stock market. These common factors define the styles that are the basis for the style benchmarks now offered by commercial providers.

The style indexes differ in construction, rules, and level of transparency. Each index constructor has a unique "take" on style, and the resulting construction method has profound implications for index performance, index fund management, active portfolio management, and asset allocation. The differences among returns of different equity styles and capitalizations (sizes) are the most surprising and powerful effects in finance. Investors would do well to consider the issues raised in this chapter before selecting a specific index for use in asset allocation, benchmarking, or performance measurement.

9. Fixed-Income Benchmarks

Fixed-income benchmarks embody a great many complex issues, of which I will touch on only a few of the most important in this chapter. After an introductory section on the basics of fixed-income benchmarks, I address two issues: the duration problem and the "bums" problem.[1] These issues arise because fixed-income benchmarks are capitalization weighted and all-inclusive. The duration problem is the fact that the duration of the benchmark comes from issuer preferences and is not necessarily the duration that a given investor should hold. The bums (or deadbeats) problem is that the biggest debtors (whether companies, countries, or other entities) have the largest weights in the benchmark.[2]

I will also comment briefly on the risk posed by the growing weight of the credit (corporate bond) component of leading benchmarks at the same time that corporate bonds themselves have become riskier.

The Complex World of Fixed-Income Benchmarks

Unlike equities, which represent ownership interests in unique businesses and which are notoriously hard to group into meaningful categories, fixed-income assets have closely specified cash flows and other properties that make them easy to classify into distinct groupings. **Exhibit 9.1** is an "index map" constructed by Lehman Brothers, a major bond dealer and the source of one of the industry's principal suites of indexes. It shows the particular Lehman benchmark for each main type of bond around the world. Note that these are the gross, not fine, divisions of the bond market; **Table 9.1** shows some (not all) of the breakdowns within one of the segments, the Lehman Brothers U.S. Aggregate Bond Index. To provide some perspective on the size of each segment, Table 9.1 also shows the market capitalization of each benchmark. (Note that the benchmarks are "nested," so you cannot add the capitalizations of the benchmarks to arrive at the capitalization of the total market.) Other index providers categorize the fixed-income market along the same lines.

---

[1]Issues that are beyond the scope of this monograph include difficulty in tracking bond benchmarks, liquidity and float, reconstitution effects and costs, differences between benchmarks and the criteria for choosing one, and currency hedging for fixed-income international benchmarks.

[2]I thank Susan A. Ollila, director of fixed-income investments at the Ford Foundation, for her helpful comments. Steve Johnson and several of his colleagues at INVESCO contributed ideas to this chapter.

Exhibit 9.1. Lehman Brothers Family of Fixed-Income Indexes

Global	U.S. and Canada	Europe	Asia
Multiverse	U.S. Universal	Pan European Universal	Asian Pacific Aggregate
Global Aggregate	U.S. Aggregate	• Euro	• Japan
• Details	• Govt/Credit	Pan European Aggregate	• Non-Japan
• Ex-JPY	• Government	• Euro-Aggregate	• Australian Dollar
• Ex-JPY ex-Securitized	• Credit	Government	Aggregate
• Ex-USD	Details	Credit	Euro Yen
• Ex-Euro	• Securitized	Details	Asia Credit
Global High Yield	• Flash Report	Securitized	Swaps
Global Treasury	U.S. High Yield	• Sterling Aggregate	Customized
Global Credit	• Details	• Swedish Krona Aggregate	
Global Securitized	Municipals	• Danish Krone Aggregate	
Global Real	Canadian	• Norwegian Krone Aggregate	
Capital Securities	Other indexes	Pan-European High Yield	
Customized	• Euro Dollar	• Details	
	• Hourly Treasury	• Euro	
	• Short Treasury	• Non-Euro	
	• Bellwethers	Swiss Franc Aggregate	
	• 144A	Danish Mortgages	
	• CMBS[a]	Swaps	
	• Private Placement	• Euro	
	• Corporate Loan	• Sterling	
	• Swaps	Customized	
	U.S. Convertibles		
	Customized		

[a]Commercial mortgage-backed securities.

Source: Lehman Brothers Global Family of Indices reprinted by permission of Lehman Brothers.

This granularity is made possible by the highly specified nature of a bond contract. The term to maturity, type of issuer, currency in which the bond pays interest and principal, priority of claims on the issuer's assets in case of insolvency, "call" or prepayment provisions, and other characteristics form the basis for an index map. Two bonds with similar characteristics will be in the same category or sub-benchmark and will also have similar returns, although no two bonds are identical. As a result, what academics sometimes call "mapping an asset into characteristic space," which refers to analytically breaking up an asset into its most elemental parts so that its returns and other properties can be accurately understood and forecasted, is not only possible but also

Table 9.1. Detailed Sector Breakdown of Lehman U.S. Aggregate, 23 April 2003

($ in millions)

Index	Market Cap	Index	Market Cap
U.S. Aggregate[a]		*Noncorporate sectors*	
Aaa	$7,946,126	Sovereign	$123,298
Aa	5,980,626	Intermediate	91,897
A	403,252	Long	31,400
Baa	818,320	Supranational	94,997
1–3 year	743,927	Intermediate	85,804
3–5 year	2,072,759	Long	9,193
5–7 year	2,272,284	Foreign agency	52,248
7–10 year	1,164,223	Intermediate	51,327
10+ year	1,262,647	Long	921
	1,174,213	Foreign local government	57,390
Sectors		Intermediate	34,538
Intermediate Aggregate	$6,782,703	Long	22,852
U.S. Govt/Credit	4,833,257		
Intermediate	3,669,835	*Securitized*	$3,112,869
Long	1,163,422	CMBS	188,138
U.S. Government	2,699,308	ABS[b]	151,641
Intermediate	2,026,225	Credit card	50,330
Long	673,083	Auto	41,325
1–3 year	984,771	Home equity	27,390
U.S. Treasury	1,686,062	Utility	18,882
Intermediate	1,129,215	Manufacturing housing	13,713
Long	556,847	Aaa only	139,785
Treasury 20+ year	209,712	MBS fixed rate[c]	2,773,090
U.S. Agency	1,013,245	GNMA[d]	451,510
Intermediate	897,010	GNMA 15 year	19,021
Long	116,236	GNMA 30 year	432,489
U.S. Credit	2,133,949	FHLMC[e]	986,911
Intermediate	1,643,610	FHLMC 15 year	286,984
Long	490,339	FHLMC 20 year	49,422
Corporate	1,806,016	FHLMC 30 year	625,636
Intermediate	1,380,044	FHLMC balloon	24,869
Long	425,972	FNMA[f]	1,334,669
Noncorporate	327,933	FNMA 15 year	328,052
Intermediate	263,566	FNMA 20 year	40,735
Long	64,367	FNMA 30 year	953,981
		FNMA balloon	11,902
Corporate sectors			
Industrial	$912,067	*Other sectors*	
Intermediate	624,495	Yankee	$503,900
Long	287,572	Intermediate	393,748
Utility	171,753	Long	110,152
Intermediate	129,219		
Long	42,534		
Financial institutions	722,196		
Intermediate	626,330		
Long	95,866		

[a]Rating grades of Moody's Investors Service.
[b]Asset-backed securities.
[c]Mortgage-backed securities.
[d]Government National Mortgage Association.
[e]Federal Home Loan Mortgage Corporation.
[f]Federal National Mortgage Association.

Source: Lehman Brothers.

relatively easy for bonds.[3] The many highly specific benchmarks enumerated in Exhibit 9.1 and Table 9.1 are the outcome of this mapping. Simply knowing the name of a benchmark provides you with a good clue as to what kinds of bonds are in it, and if you have a working understanding of what duration, credit quality, prepayment provisions, and other characteristics imply for the bond's behavior, you can deduce from the fact that a given bond is in a given benchmark most of what you need to know about that bond. (But I don't want to get carried away. A bond can, for example, have a misleading credit rating, so credit analysts can add value by avoiding overrated bonds and buying underrated ones.)

Also note that in the bond market, a single issuer typically has a number of different bond issues outstanding, with different durations and possibly other characteristics that differ from one bond issue to another. That same issuer, if it is a corporation, typically has only one class of equity shares outstanding. The reason is not only that bonds mature (making multiple issues necessary simply to provide continuous financing for the issuer's activities) but also that issuers try to take advantage of the changing shape of yield curves, quirks in regulations and tax laws, and clientele effects.

For these reasons, bond portfolio management has a very different character from equity portfolio management. There are a great many more bonds than stocks in the market.[4] Although most large-cap U.S. equity portfolios have quite a few stocks in common, bond portfolios with similar goals and attributes may not have any issues in common. And although many practitioners of equity research and portfolio management regard their activity as a mixture of art and science, bond management is mostly science, and individuals with advanced mathematical or scientific training tend to be the best at it.

Capitalization Weighting of Fixed-Income Benchmarks

Cap-weighted benchmarks have become standard for almost all asset classes, including fixed income. This practice originated with equities, for which,

---

[3]Such mapping of equity assets is a goal that generally eludes equity researchers, despite the best efforts of Barra. Researchers have attempted to map stocks into characteristic space by classifying stocks into styles, sectors, and industries. But because each stock represents ownership of a business with a great deal of idiosyncratic (nonmarket) risk and the cash flows from a stock are not well specified in advance, such groupings may contain stocks that are not like one another at all. Two aluminum companies or two insurance companies, for example, may have returns that are mostly unrelated.

[4]At least this disparity is true if you count municipal bonds. At any rate, the number of bonds that have a significant impact on the returns of cap-weighted benchmarks is considerably larger than the corresponding number of stocks.

according to the capital asset pricing model, such a benchmark is the mean–variance-efficient portfolio if you do not have special insight into the value of any particular security (see Chapter 4). Equity benchmarks are also typically all-inclusive, in the sense of containing every security that meets the criteria for inclusion; this practice also has been applied to bonds. Extending these equity-based practices to fixed-income securities makes benchmark construction easy, but it does not necessarily make the benchmark a good investment. First, the theoretical argument that the market portfolio of bonds is efficient is much more tenuous than it is for equities.[5] Second, the most highly indebted companies get the biggest benchmark weights (the bums problem). Cap-weighted, all-inclusive benchmarks are useful for performance evaluation, however, because active management against such a benchmark is a zero-sum game by definition.

All-inclusiveness has consequences for liquidity in the bond markets. In equity markets, the stocks making up the lion's share of any cap-weighted benchmark—even the very broad Wilshire 5000—are fairly liquid. The bond market, however, is almost exclusively a dealer market (that is, the investor must buy the bond from the dealer's inventory and sell the bond back to the dealer). As a result, many issues in an all-inclusive bond benchmark, especially corporate issues, are difficult to trade and price-pressure effects are substantial. Bond portfolio managers thus find tracking the benchmarks, either through sampling or full replication, to be difficult. A number of bond index funds exist, and they track the indexes well, but a fund must be very large to do so because of the large number of bonds in the benchmark and the large order sizes required to get reasonably good execution.[6]

---

[5]Stretching a point, some have argued that if the cap-weighted combination of all risky assets (not only stocks) is mean–variance efficient, as Roll (1977) said, then a cap-weighted portfolio of all outstanding bonds—which is, of course, part of the cap-weighted portfolio of all assets—is the efficient set within the fixed-income asset class. This argument is the theoretical justification for extending cap-weighted benchmarks to asset classes other than equities. For this justification to be valid, however, the assets must represent some sort of wealth in the real economy. Because offsetting claims may exist in the bond market (especially in structured debt and derivatives), which would cause double or multiple counting of wealth, and because controversy continues as to whether government bonds represent wealth (see Barro 1974), to consider the cap-weighted portfolio of bonds to be efficient is theoretically suspect. Each investor, rather than holding the cap-weighted benchmark, should seek the duration and other bond portfolio attributes that fit the investor's needs or liabilities.

[6]The observation that large order size is required to get good execution in the bond market is in contrast to the equity market, where large orders tend to be expensive to trade. See Dynkin, Hyman, and Konstantinovsky (2002).

The Duration Problem

The duration structure of a cap-weighted bond benchmark—that is, the proportions of bonds in short-, intermediate-, and long-term categories—reflects the maturity or duration preferences of issuers, who are seeking to minimize their (apparent) cost of capital.[7] Investors, however, are not trying to minimize their returns (which are the issuers' costs of capital) but to maximize returns. Moreover, an investor usually has specific time-horizon preferences that make one duration more advantageous than another. These preferences do not necessarily match those of issuers in the aggregate, whose preferences are reflected in the benchmark. This concept is expressed in the "preferred habitat theory" in the context of explaining why yield curves behave as they do.[8]

For example, defined-benefit pension plans have long-term nominal liabilities and, therefore, consider long-term bonds to be low-risk investments because the duration of the bonds roughly equals the duration of the liabilities. Because of demand from this clientele, the U.S. Treasury and other issuers need to pay only a modest yield premium for long bonds, despite the much greater volatility of these issues. The other major clientele—investors who are concerned about volatility as well as return and who have no specifically defined nominal liabilities—see long bonds as higher-risk investments and thus tend to find these bonds less attractive, at roughly the same yields, than other issues. Investors in this latter category include individuals, endowments, and foundations.

As a result, there is an optimal solution for each investor, not one optimal solution for all investors. No investor—not even one with no defined time horizon at all—should necessarily hold the benchmark duration. Because the benchmark duration is a historical accident, the optimal portfolio for an investor with no defined time horizon should be set by that investor's risk tolerance rather than by matching the duration of the benchmark.

Put another way, a duration is like a beta. It is a factor exposure. Beta is exposure to the equity market factor; duration is exposure to the interest rate factor. The choice of the duration or beta to hold is an asset-allocation decision. In equities, investors typically, and most efficiently, make such decisions by

---

[7]I say "apparent" because, according to the Modigliani and Miller (1958) invariance proposition, the cost of capital of a company is set on the asset side of the balance sheet by the risk of the company's projects (business lines), not by the way the projects are financed. The current cost of servicing debt does matter, however, in a world with transaction costs and with differential tax treatment of equity and debt. If you accept these arguments, then the role of the chief financial officer is to minimize the transaction costs and taxes associated with financing the company's operations.

[8]See Modigliani and Sutch (1969) and also, for a perspective on market efficiency under preferred habitat conditions, Mishkin (1980).

adjusting up or down the proportion of equities in their overall asset mixes, not by holding low- or high-beta stocks. In fixed income, however, adjusting the duration within the portfolio is much more practical than holding a market-duration portfolio and then "levering" the duration up or down to the desired level using cash or derivatives. Because issuers do not have to pay a great deal of yield or return premium to float long-term issues, given the demand for such issues from pension funds and other investors with long-term liabilities, duration extension does not provide much of a risk premium. This assertion is supported by the data in **Table 9.2**. In 1976–2002, the Lehman U.S. Aggregate, representing the full spectrum of maturities in the fixed-income market, outperformed the intermediate version of that benchmark by only 0.15 percentage points (pps) a year while taking appreciably more risk; as a result, the Sharpe ratio, which measures the reward per unit of risk taken, is lower for the Aggregate than for the Intermediate Aggregate. Because growth in the mortgage market greatly influenced the performance of the Aggregate in this period, the results from comparing these two indexes might be distorted. To remove the distortion, I compared the results for the Lehman Brothers Government/ Credit Bond Index and its intermediate counterpart; these indexes do not include mortgages. Table 9.2 shows the return advantage of the longer-maturity Government/Credit Index to be 0.30 pps a year, still not enough to give it a higher Sharpe ratio than the Intermediate Government/Credit Index. In other words, the slope representing the additional return per unit of duration risk taken is not steep. I found similar results when I broke the 1976–2002 period into subperiods.

Table 9.2. Summary Statistics for Performance of Leading Fixed-Income Indexes, January 1976–December 2002

Index	Compound Annual Return	Standard Deviation	Sharpe Ratio[a]
Lehman Intermediate Aggregate	9.19%	5.43%	0.512
Lehman Aggregate	9.34	6.64	0.449
Lehman Intermediate Govt/Credit	9.00	4.96	0.516
Lehman Govt/Credit	9.30	6.59	0.446
T-bills[b]	6.54	0.87	0.000

[a]Calculated with the T-bill return (see next note) as the riskless asset.
[b]U.S. T-bills with an average of 30 days remaining to maturity, from Ibbotson Associates (2003).

Sources: Lehman Brothers; Ibbotson Associates.

Thus, although investors with long-duration liabilities, such as pension funds, should hold long-duration fixed-income portfolios, most other categories of investors should avoid these bonds. Many institutional investors have addressed these concerns by adopting intermediate-duration benchmarks, such as the Lehman Brothers Intermediate Aggregate Bond Index, rather than broad market benchmarks.

The Bums Problem

Because the issuers who manage to go deepest into debt—the biggest bums—have the largest weights in a cap-weighted benchmark, such a benchmark is not likely to be mean–variance efficient. If you are tracking such a benchmark, when someone issues a security, you have to buy it in proportion to its capitalization weight to minimize tracking error to the benchmark, even if the security is only marginally of high enough quality to make it into the benchmark and even if the size of the issue, and hence its weight in the benchmark, is inordinately large. Such securities would seem to be the most likely to be downgraded or to default. The bums problem applies to countries in an international sovereign bond benchmark just as it does to corporations in a U.S. bond benchmark.

Although the bums problem is probably best appreciated relative to corporate bonds, the international sovereign bond market provides a more clearcut example of it (because the data are readily available). **Table 9.3** shows the weights of various countries in the non-U.S. component of the Citigroup World Government Bond Index (WGBI) as of early 2003.[9] By far the largest weight in the benchmark is Japan, a country that has been in a 13-year bear market involving multiple recessions (sometimes collectively referred to as a depression). A generation ago (until 1966), Japan was constitutionally forbidden to issue debt and Italy had an outsize weight in the index, at least relative to that country's economy. So, holding the benchmark seems to be a bet on whatever country has most profoundly mismanaged its public finances. This bet sometimes works out well: Italy was a strong performer because it became a developed market between 1966 and today and because "convergence" on the way to the formation of the euro caused yields to decline. But the harmonization of Europe is a once-in-a-lifetime event, maybe once in a millennium. A large position in lira-denominated bonds did not seem prudent in the 1960s, and a 35 percent position in yen-denominated bonds does not seem prudent now.

---

[9]Formerly, this index was maintained by Salomon Smith Barney.

Table 9.3. Country Weights of Non-U.S. Component of Citigroup WGBI, 20 February 2003

Country	Weight
Australia	0.4%
Belgium	3.8
Canada	3.0
Denmark	1.2
France	10.2
Germany	11.3
Italy	12.1
Japan	35.1
Netherlands	2.8
Spain	4.6
Sweden	0.8
United Kingdom	8.0
Others	6.8

Source: Citigroup.

Credit Market Growth and Volatility

A final issue related to fixed-income benchmarks arises from the recent growth in the size of the credit (corporate bond) market at a time when corporate bonds were individually becoming riskier. The interaction of these two factors has caused broad bond benchmarks (the Lehman Aggregate, Lehman Government/Credit, and so forth) to be riskier today than they were historically.

Table 9.4 shows the changing composition of four such benchmarks. Although the trend over the very long term is the displacement of corporate bonds by mortgage-backed securities (MBS) and asset-backed securities (ABS), which bond managers collectively refer to as "mortgages," the more recent trend is a reduction in the size of U.S. Treasury debt and an increase in corporate issues. With $2.2 trillion of the perhaps $5 trillion U.S. corporate bond market having been downgraded in just the two years of 2001 and 2002, the absolute risk in these benchmarks was at or near an all-time high in the fall of 2002, as shown by the yield spread of the Lehman Brothers Credit Bond Index over the Treasury market in **Figure 9.1.** Although the market then rallied (yield spreads declined), the credit market is still volatile. This is not your father's fixed-income benchmark.

Table 9.4. Changing Composition of Bond Benchmarks

Index	1976	1986	1991	1996	1997	1998	1999	2000	2001	2002
Lehman Govt/Credit										
Treasury	35%	64%	65%	65%	62%	56%	52%	44%	36%	36%
Agency	17	11	10	9	10	12	14	18	19	20
Credit	46	25	24	26	28	32	34	38	45	44
Lehman Aggregate										
Treasury	32%	48%	45%	45%	43%	38%	33%	27%	22%	21%
Agency	15	8	7	7	7	8	9	11	11	12
MBS/ABS	11	25	31	31	31	32	36	38	39	40
Credit	42	19	17	18	19	22	22	24	27	26
Lehman Intermediate Govt/Credit										
Treasury	56%	69%	69%	67%	65%	56%	50%	39%	32%	31%
Agency	24	15	12	10	10	14	17	21	23	24
Credit	20	16	19	23	25	29	33	40	45	45
Lehman Intermediate Aggregate										
Treasury	51%	48%	41%	42%	39%	33%	27%	21%	17%	16%
Agency	22	10	7	6	6	9	9	11	12	13
MBS/ABS	18	11	12	14	15	17	18	21	24	24
Credit	9	30	40	38	39	41	45	47	46	47

Notes: Data for 2002 are as of 29 June; data for other years are as of 31 December. Columns do not sum to 100 percent because of rounding.

Source: Lehman Brothers. Table data originally appeared in Johnson and Siegel (2003).

At the same time that corporate bond exposure has made broad fixed-income benchmarks riskier, many fixed-income managers have begun trading bonds like equities—instead of buying and holding them to maturity, as they did a generation ago. This change in behavior is a result of the existence and popularity of cap-weighted fixed-income benchmarks. Increasingly, fixed-income managers regard their job as maximizing active return subject to a penalty for active risk, which is exactly what I suggested in Chapter 2 that they should be doing. This practice is potentially in conflict, however, with the goals of those fixed-income investors who regard bonds as vehicles for capital preservation, not total return. If you hold bonds as an "anchor to windward"—that is, an investment that preserves its value (and pays a fixed income) while having a low correlation with other assets (such as equities)—maybe you should take less duration risk (and less credit risk) than is found in broad-market bond benchmarks.[10]

---

[10]Although a given bond pays a fixed income, a bond portfolio (or bond mutual fund) does not because of reinvestment risk and changing portfolio composition. Every once in a while, a reminder to investors of why fixed-income assets are so called is helpful.

Figure 9.1. Yield Spread of Lehman Credit over Treasury Index, 1989–2002

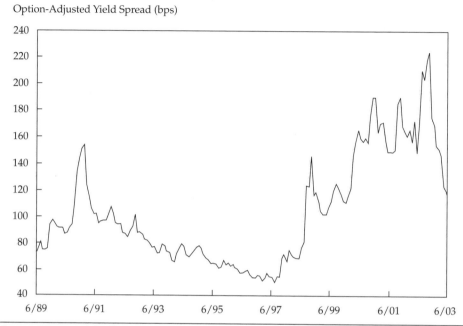

Source: Figure originally appeared in Johnson and Siegel (2003); updated by the author using Lehman Brothers data.

Conclusion

Cap-weighted fixed-income benchmarks are a bit of a puzzle. Although they represent the investment opportunities in the asset class, they are unlikely to be an ideal portfolio for any given investor. Nevertheless, active fixed-income management is a zero-sum game relative to a well-constructed cap-weighted benchmark, so performance evaluation can sensibly be conducted by comparing manager returns with benchmark returns—as long as you can simultaneously focus on what the purpose of the fixed-income investment was in the first place.

10. International Equity Benchmarks

International (that is, non-U.S.) equity benchmarks differ from U.S. equity benchmarks in some distinct ways:[1]
- Float adjustment is much more important for international stocks.
- The convention is to divide international equity markets into developed and emerging categories, and the decision as to which countries belong in which category has consequences for both the benchmarks and the countries' markets.
- An investor/manager must keep track of currencies and construct both local-currency and investor-currency versions of the benchmark.

Expressing benchmark returns in more than one currency is straightforward. Float adjustment and the division of the world into developed and emerging markets, however, are sources of controversy.

The discussion in this chapter will focus on international equity benchmarks from the viewpoint of U.S. investors. I will also review the trade-offs involved in international equity index construction and touch on the impact of benchmarking in international markets.

Early Development of Indexes

Stock indexes around the world, including the United States, were first typically compiled by newspapers. Examples include the Dow Jones in the United States, the Nikkei in Japan, the DAX in Germany, and the *Financial Times* indexes in the United Kingdom. Such indexes were price-only (not total-return) indexes and were generally not capitalization weighted. Academic or broker-age-affiliated researchers also created stock indexes in some countries.[2] But although stock indexes already existed in a number of countries long before the mid-1960s, the first usable benchmarks were initiated by Nilly Sikorsky of

---

[1] I thank Mark Sladkus of Morgan Stanley Capital International for providing an interview used in this chapter, and I thank Steven Schoenfeld of Active Index Advisors for sharing many of the ideas and much of the data in Schoenfeld and Ginis (2002). Schoenfeld was at Barclays Global Investors when he did the work referred to in this chapter.

[2] For an excellent general discussion of global equity returns and indexes and a 101-year historical reconstruction in 16 countries based on returns from various carefully documented sources, see Dimson, Marsh, and Staunton (2002).

the Capital Group in November 1968.[3] Unlike most inventors who struggle to capitalize on their inventions, the Capital Group's successor company in index construction, Morgan Stanley Capital International (MSCI), became and has remained the dominant provider of international equity indexes.[4]

The Capital Group constructed the MSCI benchmarks to help investors measure active management performance. (Index funds had not been invented yet.) Unlike earlier efforts, the MSCI indexes followed the basic principles of good index construction—market-cap weighting, publication of constituent lists, and historical reconstruction of data so that they would be useful for analyzing asset allocation. These indexes did, however, have one quirk: They sought to capture only 60 percent of the market cap of the countries and sectors they covered. This percentage was small even by the modest standards of the time. MSCI justified this limited capitalization coverage on liquidity grounds and decided that it would be more consistent to have one capitalization coverage standard for all countries rather than cover a larger percentage of capitalization in the more liquid countries, such as the United States and the United Kingdom.

The emergence of international equity indexes of reasonable quality (that is, indexes that were good enough to double as practical benchmarks) meshed nicely with a trend toward internationalization of portfolios that had been developing in the 1970s and that came to the forefront in the 1980s. International portfolios had been available to U.S. investors for a long time, mostly from European managers, such as Robeco. In the late 1970s and early 1980s, however, U.S. investors began to perceive their home country as having inferior economic performance and began more aggressively to seek higher rates of return in booming Japanese, German, and other non-U.S. markets.

U.S. investors in the late 1970s and the 1980s were also influenced by a number of academic studies showing that international investing had delivered a risk premium (Solnik 1974; Bergstrom 1975). Although international stocks had outperformed U.S. stocks in the historical period for which data were available, some investors (and academics) naively interpreted the results of these studies as meaning that international stocks would permanently offer a risk premium in the future. I have always been puzzled by this train of thought: Investors in any country might see investing in countries other than their own as risky. In other words, they might have a "home country bias," so

---

[3]See Sikorsky (1982). The November 1968 date represents a test launch, and the indexes were backdated to 1959. The eventual MSCI indexes had an initiation and base date of 1 January 1970.

[4]Sikorsky is president of Capital International S.A., an operating unit of the Capital Group; MSCI is a joint venture of Morgan Stanley and Capital International and is now controlled by Morgan Stanley.

they would require a higher return to entice them to invest in a different country. But that logic works both ways: U.S. investors would require a risk premium to invest in non-U.S. markets and non-U.S. investors would require a premium to invest in the United States. If the markets are roughly the same size (and they are), the two premiums should cancel each other out.[5] Investors should invest internationally for many reasons—for diversification and because the industrial mix of every country is different—but capturing a risk premium is not one of them.

Where there are portfolios, there need to be benchmarks. During this same period, the MSCI EAFE Index was pretty much the only international equity index available, so it became the almost universal standard for international equity benchmarks.[6] It remains so even though EAFE omits Canada and another index using the same methodology (the MSCI World ex-U.S Index) that includes Canada has been available for quite some time.

Need for Float Adjustment

In the late 1980s, the Japanese equity market entered a super-boom phase that caused the weight of Japan in EAFE to soar to almost 60 percent by the end of 1989. The implications of this development for portfolio management were peculiar. As Japanese stocks took on higher and higher multiples, they became less and less attractive to most fundamentals-oriented active managers. To minimize tracking error to the benchmark, however—and to stay even with the benchmark's performance, which was boosted by its large weight in Japan—portfolio managers had to hold larger and larger Japanese equity positions.

Part of Japan's large weight in EAFE was a result of growth of the country's real economy and was, therefore, justified on fundamental grounds. And part of the large weight was caused by the high multiples that prevailed in the Japanese market. But part of the weight was the result of a large volume of cross-holdings in Japan. In cross-holding, one company owns shares of another, so including the full capitalization of both companies in an index is double counting. In addition, many shares were closely held, so they were unavailable to the public even if they did not represent cross-holdings.

To correct these problems, some managers tried to persuade clients to use either an "EAFE light" benchmark with an artificially reduced weight in

---

[5]For the two premiums to cancel each other out, U.S. and non-U.S. investors would also need roughly the same amount of aversion to the risk represented by investing in each other's markets.

[6]Originally, "EAFE" stood for Europe/Australia/Far East Index. Later, the name was changed to the Europe/Australasia/Far East Index.

Japan or a benchmark weighted by gross domestic product. Free-float adjustment, however, seemed to be a more natural solution.[7]

Salomon–Russell was the first organization (that I know of) to introduce float-adjusted benchmarks. Although the Salomon–Russell (now Citigroup) indexes did not attract a large market share because of the reluctance of sponsors and managers to change benchmarks, the superiority of its methodology was widely recognized. As a result, all the indexes introduced by new providers were float adjusted. Finally, after years of preparation, MSCI converted its indexes to a float-adjusted basis on 31 May 2002. Some details of this conversion and its effect on market prices are discussed later in this chapter. In the meantime, note the differences in capitalizations and weights between MSCI's full-capitalization and free-float indexes shown in **Table 10.1**.

When Japanese stocks were rising in the 1980s, managers struggled to stay even with full-cap benchmarks, and as Japanese stocks plunged in the 1990s, they found the full-cap indexes easy to beat. (With all benchmarks now float adjusted and with Japan constituting only 21 percent of EAFE as of March 2003, managers may not find that benchmark as easy to beat in the future.) When a benchmark is either very easy or very difficult for a large proportion of managers to beat, something is probably wrong with the benchmark—not with the theory that says active management is a zero-sum game!

The question of full-capitalization versus float-adjusted benchmarks is still a source of controversy for the U.S. equity market. For international equity benchmarks, however, the question has been resolved. Although the precise nature of the float adjustment varies from provider to provider (see Schoenfeld and Ginis 2002), no international equity benchmark uses full capitalization anymore.

International Equity Indexes Compared

Today, major providers of international equity indexes include MSCI, Citigroup, FTSE, Standard & Poor's, and Dow Jones and Company. **Exhibit 10.1** presents the basic characteristics of each index and provides a brief description of how each suite of indexes is constructed. Schoenfeld and Ginis described in detail how each of these indexes is constructed, enumerated the key criteria by which a good international index can be identified, and rated each index according to each of the criteria.

---

[7] Free-float weighting does not eliminate distortions caused by high market prices (valuations), as it should not if a cap-weighted benchmark is the goal.

Table 10.1. Composition of MSCI Float-Adjusted and Full-Cap World Indexes, 30 November 2001

Country	MSCI World Provisional Index (float adjusted, 85% cap coverage)			MSCI World Index (full cap, 60% cap coverage)		
	No. of Companies	Market Cap (millions)	Index Weight	No. of Companies	Market Cap (millions)	Index Weight
Australia	71	$ 243,658	1.54%	53	$ 236,243	1.50%
Austria	12	6,580	0.04	15	12,545	0.08
Belgium	17	50,496	0.32	16	70,735	0.45
Canada	86	336,853	2.13	68	340,053	2.16
Denmark	25	45,338	0.29	19	67,676	0.43
Finland	21	143,153	0.91	27	143,997	0.92
France	54	577,055	3.66	50	773,886	4.92
Germany	50	426,671	2.70	45	567,913	3.61
Greece	23	24,711	0.16	23	24,711	0.16
Hong Kong	28	99,401	0.63	28	143,944	0.91
Ireland	14	54,775	0.35	13	48,108	0.31
Italy	42	218,979	1.39	40	312,164	1.98
Japan	322	1,295,698	8.21	274	1,526,191	9.70
Netherlands	25	350,249	2.22	23	386,266	2.46
New Zealand	15	8,047	0.05	11	9,187	0.06
Norway	25	27,141	0.17	21	34,682	0.22
Portugal	10	23,418	0.15	10	37,240	0.24
Singapore	35	45,494	0.29	28	58,947	0.37
Spain	27	206,809	1.31	31	226,677	1.44
Sweden	38	137,015	0.87	34	167,619	1.07
Switzerland	38	467,962	2.97	35	491,214	3.12
United Kingdom	137	1,718,828	10.89	111	1,591,282	10.11
United States	413	9,270,878	58.75	322	8,462,332	53.79
Total	1,528	$15,779,217	100.00%	1,297	$15,733,613	100.00%

Source: MSCI.

Trade-Offs in Constructing International Indexes. As discussed for the domestic equity indexes, constructing any benchmark involves trade-offs, but the trade-offs differ somewhat from one asset class to another. Trade-offs discussed in this section are specific to international equity benchmarks or have special resonance when a U.S. investor is deciding which international equity benchmark to use (for more, see Schoenfeld and Ginis).

■ *Breadth vs. investability.* International indexes face a direct trade-off between breadth (the number of different stocks in an index) and investability. (An index is investable to the extent that you can readily buy and sell the stocks

Exhibit 10.1. Basic Characteristics of Major International Equity Benchmarks, 30 June 2002

Provider	Index	Country Coverage	No. of Securities	No. of Countries	Target Market Cap by Country (%)	Historical Inception Date
MSCI	All Country World Index ex-U.S.	Integrated	1,799	48	85	Jan 1988
MSCI	World ex-U.S.	Developed markets	1,101	22	85	Jan 1970
MSCI	EAFE	Developed markets	1,021	21	85	Jan 1970
FTSE	All-World ex-U.S.	Integrated	1,815	48	85–90	Jan 1994
FTSE	World Developed ex-North America	Developed markets	1,294	21	85–90	Jan 1994
Citigroup	Broad Market Index Global ex-U.S.	Integrated	4,875	49	95	Jul 1989
Citigroup	Primary Markets Index—Europe Pacific	Developed markets	663	21	95	Jul 1989
Citigroup	Global 1200 ex-U.S.	Modified integrated[a]	700	30	70 (by region)	Oct 1989
Dow Jones	Global ex-U.S.	Modified integrated[a]	2,200	33	70 (by region)	Jan 1992

Note: "Integrated" indexes include developed and emerging markets.

[a]Includes advanced emerging markets.

Sources: Schoenfeld and Ginis and data collected by the author.

in it with a minimum of price-pressure effects and other transaction costs.) With international indexes—not only emerging market but also developed country indexes—the illiquidity of the smallest-cap and most closely held stocks is a greater problem than in the United States. Although most indexes exclude the smallest, least liquid securities, when selecting a benchmark you might want to take the extra measure of choosing an index that errs on the side of less breadth and greater liquidity (see Exhibit 10.1 for the number of stocks in each index). For example, the manager of an index fund with substantial cash flows in and out might not want the job of holding all 2,200 stocks in the Dow Jones Global ex-U.S. Index.

■ *Liquidity and crossing opportunities vs. index reconstitution effects.* Indexes that are most popular and most widely used as benchmarks or as the basis for index funds have greater index-level liquidity—that is, liquidity for investors seeking to buy or sell an index fund position or an actively managed position whose contents resemble, at least to some degree, those of the index. Of particular interest to institutional investors are crossing opportunities in such indexes. Crossing is the process by which an investment manager matches its own clients' buy and sell orders without using a broker and without incurring the transaction costs associated with brokerage. Crossing avoids transaction costs except for a small fee paid to the investment management firm doing the crossing.

Program trades, sometimes called portfolio trades, are another way that investors can buy or sell indexed or "benchmarked" positions. Program trades involve a broker bidding on the right to buy or sell a whole portfolio at an agreed-on price. A popular and liquid benchmark results in a lower bid from the broker because the broker's own costs are lower for such a benchmark.

Popular indexes—domestic and international—suffer, however, from index reconstitution (inclusion and deletion) effects. These effects, which I noted in Chapter 6, consist of upward price pressure on stocks chosen for inclusion in an index and downward price pressure on stocks taken out of the index. The size of the effect on a portfolio manager is, logically, proportional to the amount of assets indexed or benchmarked to the particular index. Reconstitution effects are detrimental to performance, although the underperformance does not show up in conventional performance evaluation as a negative alpha because the reconstitution effect affects the benchmark as well as the investor's actual portfolio.

Indexes with more index-level liquidity and crossing opportunities may have poorer performance because of reconstitution effects. Of the developed country equity indexes, MSCI EAFE provides by far the most opportunity to investors seeking to cross trades or otherwise take advantage of index-level liquidity, and it is also the most likely to suffer from reconstitution effects because it is the most popular index.[8]

▪ *Precise float adjustment vs. transaction costs from rebalancing.* As noted, float adjustment for international equity indexes is no longer a matter of controversy. All the indexes are float adjusted in one way or another. In international markets, however, where float adjustment has a large effect on the constituent weights, the exact method of adjustment makes a difference. Indexes that make precise float adjustments and that revise these adjustments frequently impose higher transaction costs on those benchmarking against them than indexes that use float bands or broad categories. Float bands are categories of, say, 15–25 percent, 25–50 percent, 50–75 percent, and 75–100 percent, in which the percentage represents the portion of a company's full capitalization that the index constructors regard as freely floating. Citigroup makes precise float adjustments, whereas MSCI and FTSE use bands. Float

---

[8]Although not specifically discussed in previous chapters, this trade-off also applies to the U.S. equity market and should be taken into consideration when selecting a U.S. equity benchmark.

bands make sense because transaction costs are a real loss to the investor; what is to be gained by replicating the float of the market exactly is not as clear.

■ *Objectivity and transparency vs. judgment.* Objective and clearly stated rules for index construction convey as large an advantage to international equity indexes as to U.S. indexes. They enable both index funds and active managers to predict what will be in the benchmark and, as a result, to trade more effectively in anticipation of changes in benchmark contents. They also make benchmarks easier to understand and to use as proxies for asset classes in asset allocation.

From this perspective, MSCI's judgment-based method for constructing EAFE and its other indexes is difficult to defend (as is S&P's use of an index committee to construct the S&P 500). When MSCI's indexes contained (by design) only 60 percent of the capitalization of each country and sector, however, it had little choice but to use judgment to select the companies. An odd result of this situation was that the MSCI U.S. index did not contain Ford Motor Company because General Motors Corporation accounted for more than 60 percent of the U.S. automotive sector and "crowded out" the other U.S. auto companies, even mega-cap Ford. Thus, a manager using the MSCI U.S. index as a benchmark would have incurred tracking error simply by holding Ford at its market-cap weight. Now that MSCI's indexes capture 85 percent of capitalization, MSCI's use of judgment to pick the stocks has less impact on index contents.

The advantages of benchmarking to a widely accepted index, such as EAFE or the S&P 500, include ease of communication and a high degree of index-level liquidity, which may overcome the disadvantages associated with using a judgment-based index.

Style/Size Indexes. The size and value–growth distinctions are as important for international equities as they are in the U.S. market.[9] Of the index constructors shown in Exhibit 10.1, MSCI and Citigroup calculate style and size subindexes. The MSCI indexes, in particular, also have a substantial back history, which is helpful for understanding and comparing style effects in various countries. These effects are at least as dramatic outside the U.S. market as within it.

An understanding of the specific construction methods of the subindexes is important before attempting to use them as benchmarks or buying index funds based on them. Describing them is beyond the scope of this monograph, but you can find information on international style indexes in Schoenfeld and Ginis.

---

[9]For a full discussion of the size effect internationally, see Clothier, Waring, and Siegel (1998).

Classification of Countries as Developed or Emerging

The division of non-U.S. markets into developed and emerging categories dates back to 1981 when Antoine van Agtmael, an investment manager at the World Bank, referred (in a flash of marketing brilliance) to what were then called third-world or developing countries as emerging markets (Thomas 1999). Mark Mobius of the Franklin Templeton (then, simply Templeton) organization was among the other managers who quickly capitalized on the trend to invest in countries, such as the Asian tigers, Mexico, Brazil, and (later) the formerly communist countries of Central and Eastern Europe, that were not in any established equity benchmark.[10] The emergence of China as a capitalist society in the 1990s reinforced the level of interest in (although not the performance of) emerging markets, and Russia and India are now having an impact. With the rising interest of institutional investors in the emerging markets came the need for benchmarks, so a number of index providers stepped up to the plate to provide them.

The first emerging market benchmarks were provided by the International Finance Corporation (IFC) and Baring Securities (now ING Barings). Soon afterward, MSCI and Citigroup constructed emerging market indexes. MSCI's Emerging Markets Free Index (EMF) gained an early popular lead, just as MSCI's EAFE had for developed markets. (The "free" in EMF refers not to free float but to the ability of investors from outside a given country to transact freely in that country's market. Such freedom includes the unrestricted exchange of currencies and movement of capital across borders.)

Today, the leading providers of emerging market benchmarks are the same as the leading providers of developed market benchmarks identified in Exhibit 10.1. The Barings indexes have been folded into the FTSE, and the IFC indexes have been folded into the Standard & Poor's series of indexes. All of the providers shown in Exhibit 10.1 also constructed integrated (that is, developed + emerging markets) indexes.

Boundary between Developed and Emerging Markets. When an index constructor decides that a country is going to be in the developed category or the emerging category, that decision has consequences for the characteristics of the benchmark and, potentially, for the country itself. First, the index constructor may be undecided about where to put the country

---

[10]The traditional "Asian tigers" were Hong Kong, South Korea, Singapore, and Taiwan; later, the term was sometimes expanded to include Malaysia, Thailand, and other countries. Mexico was in the original MSCI suite of indexes discussed in Sikorsky (1982). The former communist countries were typically not strangers to equity investing; Hungary, for example, had the world's fourth largest stock exchange in 1900.

because the country's market capitalization is large relative to an emerging market index. For example, South Korea's equity market is in the MSCI EMF and other emerging market indexes, but its market is quite well developed and has a capitalization of $100.7 billion, equal to 19.9 percent of the EMF. Thus, the decision to include or exclude Korea in the EMF had a real impact on the average company size and average level of country development in that index. As a constituent of EAFE (which it is scheduled to become), Korea will be a small rather than a huge player.

For the country, being in a developed index is highly desirable because far more assets are committed to developed than to emerging markets. For example, Korean companies would rather have a small weight in EAFE than a large weight in the EMF. This preference reflects the fact that when a country graduates from MSCI's emerging markets indexes to EAFE, as Portugal, Greece, Ireland, and many other countries have done and as Korea may do soon, a new source of capital becomes available to that country's companies. Inclusion in a broadly followed index of developed countries, in itself, makes a country more developed.

Acceptance of Integrated Indexes. There is no compelling reason why international managers should segregate themselves into developed and emerging markets specialists or why clients should establish separate allocations to these categories of markets. A historical reason is the desire of clients (investors) to reassure themselves that they are not taking undue risk. They pursued this goal by investing only in developed markets believed to have transparent accounting rules, liquid exchanges, and stable currencies. Investors also sought to avoid capital-control risk by holding only developed market securities. Today, however, the largest companies in the emerging markets are traded on the New York Stock Exchange and are thus free of capital-control risk (as well as subject to the exchange's transparency and liquidity standards). And some of these companies are globally dominant in their industries. Therefore, the developed–emerging distinction seems less important than it once was and investment managers increasingly find that the skills used to identify attractive stocks play equally well in developed and emerging economies.

As a result, integrated mandates (mandates for a single manager to invest in all non-U.S. markets, whether developed or emerging) are growing rapidly. Schoenfeld and Ginis reported that 48 percent of all new international mandates in the first half of 2002 were for integrated portfolios, up from 20 percent in 2000 and 13.6 percent in 1999.[11] The benchmark for such mandates is typically the MSCI All Country World Index ex-U.S.

---

[11]Schoenfeld and Ginis were citing data from InterSec Research Corporation.

Impact of Benchmarking on International Markets

The impact of inclusion of a stock in a benchmark on that stock's price has been less thoroughly studied in international markets than in the United States. Two recent events, however, offer evidence on the consequences of benchmarking for international markets.

The Odd Case of Malaysia. Up to 1998, Malaysia was a constituent of both the EAFE and EMF indexes because of an odd historical situation. The countries of Singapore and Malaysia were united until 1965, and their stock exchanges developed as a unit in the early 1970s (even after the countries separated politically), when MSCI was contemplating adding a number of countries to the developed market EAFE index. Singapore was clearly a developed country, but no separate MSCI Singapore index existed, only a Singapore/Malaysia index. In a press release, Capital International, which at the time was the constructor of the MSCI indexes, later explained:

> Although the two markets became increasingly independent, the joint MSCI Singapore/Malaysia Index remained a constituent of the EAFE index for the next 20 years (to avoid disruption to the index, and to the markets). In May 1993, the MSCI Singapore/Malaysia index was finally split into two separate indexes. At that time, in view of Malaysia's long history of inclusion in the MSCI EAFE index, it was decided that it would remain, temporarily, in both the [EAFE and EMF] series.[12]

The result was a double-counting situation in which an investor who held one portfolio benchmarked to EAFE and another benchmarked to the EMF would receive a double weight in Malaysia (the only country in the world in this position). As of 2 September 1998, Malaysia represented 0.37 percent of EAFE and 4.40 percent of the EMF.

Then, in the wake of the Asian financial crisis of 1998, Malaysia imposed capital controls, motivating MSCI to remove that country from EAFE as of 30 September 1998. Capital International stated, "In light of the recent developments in Malaysia, it is time to put an end to this transition period."

If Malaysia had been removed from EAFE to avoid double counting at a time when no externally caused turmoil was occurring in the markets, researchers would have had a noteworthy experimental condition. They could have observed how the change in demand from indexing and benchmarking affected the Malaysian stock index relative to the stock indexes of other, roughly comparable countries, such as Thailand and Indonesia. The imposition of capital controls that spurred MSCI to make the index change, however, also ruined the experiment: Investors wanted to flee Malaysian stocks for reasons having nothing to do with their exclusion from EAFE.

---

[12]This quotation and the next one are from "Malaysia to Be Removed from MSCI EAFE," Capital International press release, 4 September 1998: www.msci.com/pressreleases/archive/pr199809a.html.

Nevertheless, if only to satisfy curiosity, I've compared the returns on Malaysian stocks with stocks and indexes for the relevant period, 1998–2000, as shown in **Figure 10.1**. Because the decision to remove Malaysia from EAFE was announced on 4 September 1998 and was to take effect on 30 September of the same year, you can see the effects of the decision by looking at returns in September and October 1998. For September 1998, Malaysia did not have the lowest return in Southeast Asia; in October 1998, it had the lowest return in the region but the return was positive. Thus, without conducting any statistical tests but simply by inspecting the results visually, you can see that the returns for Malaysia appear to have been not much different from those for other countries in the region. Malaysia's returns are also not much different from those for the broad EMF in the period surrounding Malaysia's removal from EAFE.[13]

On 30 November 1998, MSCI also removed Malaysia from the EMF because of the capital controls. When Malaysia was restored to the EMF on 23 May 2000, it had already experienced huge gains (to more than four times the 1998 low in U.S. dollar terms) and was, in fact, at a high that it still has not surpassed.[14] Either investors had been buying Malaysian stocks in anticipation of its reintroduction to the EMF or investors were ignoring Malaysia's absence from it. There was no measurable Malaysian EAFE deletion effect and there was no measurable Malaysian EMF inclusion effect.

The Biggest Index Change Ever. Recognizing that international investors had long held a strong preference for float-adjusted benchmarks and that they had sustained their loyalty to MSCI largely because of the difficulties that sponsors and managers have in switching benchmarks, MSCI converted its indexes to a float-adjusted format in a stepwise process. The process began on 31 May 2001, when the Provisional indexes were introduced. These float-adjusted indexes captured 85 percent of the capitalization of each country and of each country's industrial sectors, and they were designed to run in parallel with the Standard or original indexes for a year. (Recall that the original indexes, which were not float adjusted, captured 60 percent of capitalization by country and sector.) After a year—that is, on 31 May 2002—the Standard

---

[13]On a daily basis, the results are quite confusing. The volatile MSCI Malaysia Index actually rose, in U.S. dollars, by 75.0 percent between 1 September and 7 September 1998. By 30 September, it had fallen back to its old low. Currency depreciation was responsible for part of the decline after 7 September but had almost no impact on the 1–7 September advance. The reasons for these dramatic price moves might be a fruitful research topic for those interested in index-inclusion effects (or the effects of capital controls).

[14]As of 30 June 2003.

Figure 10.1. Cumulative Returns on Malaysian and Other Equity Markets, 1998–2000

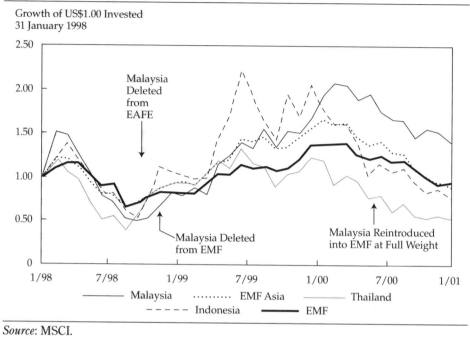

Growth of US$1.00 Invested
31 January 1998

Source: MSCI.

indexes were to be discontinued and the Provisional indexes would become the permanent MSCI indexes.

This procedure was designed to allow investors to adjust to the new index construction methods. Both the demand side—index funds and benchmark-sensitive active funds—and the supply side—brokers, hedge funds, and active managers seeking to profit from providing liquidity to the demand side—had plenty of opportunity to observe how the new indexes were constructed and what their constituents would be and to trade in anticipation of the full changeover on 31 May 2002.

Note that the conversion from full capitalization to free float and from 60 percent to 85 percent capitalization coverage affected the MSCI index weight of most of the large- and mid-cap stocks in the world. It was, to borrow the title of a Barclays Global Investors report, "the world's biggest index change ever."[15] Although little of the U.S. equity market is indexed or benchmarked to the MSCI U.S. Index, a large portion of non-U.S. equities are indexed or benchmarked to EAFE or to other MSCI indexes.

---

[15]Unpublished report, Barclays Global Investors, San Francisco (14 December 2001).

One way to measure the success of this effort is by the return differential, or spread, between the Provisional and Standard indexes (both overall and country by country). As liquidity suppliers bought stocks in the Provisional index in the hope of later selling them to indexed or benchmarked investors whose Standard index was about to be abandoned, the Provisional index should have earned an incremental return over the Standard one. In other words, the Provisional-to-Standard spread would be a measure of the transaction costs being paid by investors in the Standard index.

The original forecast was that investors could lose well over 1 percent in performance through transaction costs and/or by not switching benchmarks, Barclays noted.[16] The overall Provisional–Standard spread for the year ended 31 May 2002, however, was only 0.32 percent for the flagship EAFE index. "The World spread finished in negative territory," according to Barclays. Thus, much of the transaction cost that might have been paid was instead avoided through careful planning and a high degree of index transparency.

Results differed, of course, from country to country, and the spreads did not line up cleanly with the amount by which a country gained or lost share in EAFE and other broad indexes. For example, the United Kingdom, the country whose weight in EAFE increased the most as a result of the transition, had a generally strong market (it beat EAFE) and might have also been expected to have a high Provisional–Standard spread (because of a perceived "shortage" of U.K. stocks), but the spread actually turned out to be negative. Japan, the country that lost the most from the transition, had weak markets and might also have been expected to have a negative spread (because of a "glut" of Japanese stocks), but the spread turned out to be close to zero.[17]

Interestingly, in the first half of the transition year, the Provisional–Standard spread dove into negative territory because liquidity providers, reacting to the information in the Provisional with enthusiasm (also known as greed), grossly overestimated the demand for the stocks they were buying whereas investors on the demand side seemed confused or indifferent. Later in the transition, however, liquidity providers appeared to lose enthusiasm while demand-side investors were coming under increasing pressure to move to the weights in the Provisional indexes. So, the spread turned positive.

---

[16]This and the following quotation are from "The MSCI Reconstitution: What Happened?" Unpublished report, Barclays Global Investors, San Francisco (2002).

[17]I use quote marks to describe "shortages" and "gluts" in this context because in open markets, supply–demand imbalances (shortages and gluts) exist only at the current price; the imbalance is resolved by a change in price that calls forth additional supply or that removes some of the excess supply.

The lessons of this episode are not only that investors, managers, and index constructors can cooperate to avoid unnecessary transaction costs but also that markets appear to "work" quite well at the micro level (if the word micro can be used to describe this vast and complex change in an industry-dominant benchmark). They work, that is, to provide liquidity with a reasonable degree of efficiency when it is needed and to make transaction costs, which could have been huge and unpredictable, quite small.

11. Hedge Fund Benchmarks

The idea that hedge funds need benchmarks (or that their clients need them) is new and surprising.[1] Originally, hedge funds were the preserve of wealthy families. Later, a number of endowments, foundations, and other institutional investors added hedge funds in the belief that managers left to their own devices and freed from the constraints implied by benchmarks would achieve superior performance—perhaps even performance uncorrelated with the overall movements of markets.

Hedge fund investing incorporates several threads, all of which are hostile to benchmarking. One thread is the goal of capital preservation: A strategy intended to avoid losses will also sharply curtail gains when markets are rising if the value added through active management skill is less than exceptional. Short selling (of index futures as well as of securities believed to be overpriced) is a principal strategy in funds managed with such a goal. A second, contrasting, thread is the pursuit of high performance: Some investors wish to make as much money as possible, often in highly undiversified and/or leveraged strategies; short selling is also often part of these strategies. With most high-performance strategies, a benchmarking approach would impose a large penalty for taking active risk; it would require a fund's active return to be extraordinary to justify holding the fund. A third thread, woven into the first two, is a belief in pure manager skill, that is, the idea that the essence of active management can be distilled by removing all market influences; thus, traditional asset class benchmarks do not have much relevance to hedge funds.

It is thus a testament to the power of consultants, clients, and the intellectual appeal of performance measurement and evaluation that hedge fund benchmarks emerged at all. Although I doubt that hedge fund managers wanted to be "benchmarked," the desire to measure how managers are doing was too strong for hedge fund managers to resist.[2] As a result, several suites of hedge fund benchmarks—generally consisting of a number of style

---

[1]The author thanks Elizabeth Hilpman of Barlow Partners and Thomas Schneeweis of the Center for International Securities and Derivatives Markets at the University of Massachusetts for helpful comments.

[2]Naturally, the creators of hedge fund benchmarks have sought to avoid incorporating the traditional market influences (the stock market, bond market, and so forth) while uncovering new ones with greater potential relevance.

subcategories as well as an overall index—had been created by early 2003. Among the providers are Zurich Capital Markets (ZCM), CSFB/Tremont (Credit Suisse First Boston/Tremont), Evaluation Associates Capital Markets (EACM), Standard & Poor's, and Morgan Stanley Capital International. This chapter focuses on the ZCM benchmarks.[3]

Hedge Fund Benchmark Construction

Unlike traditional asset-class benchmarks, for which capitalization weighting is a virtual prerequisite for the index to be acceptable, most hedge fund benchmarks are equally weighted. (CSFB/Tremont is cap weighted, with the assets under management in the funds as the "capitalizations.") With hedge funds, cap weighting makes limited sense: The capitalizations of stocks, bonds, and other primary assets contain economic information because they are the market's appraisal of a business or a stream of cash flows, but the capitalizations of hedge funds themselves contain little information. They reflect only the amount that investors have entrusted to one manager rather than another. After all, hedge funds are portfolios, not companies.[4]

Survivor Bias. Hedge fund indexes typically try to avoid survivor bias by including in the index return the final return for hedge funds that have ceased to exist. Avoiding survivor bias is important because the hedge funds that go out of business, or that simply stop reporting their performance, tend to be those that have poor returns. (A few funds stop reporting because they have become closed to new investment, which usually reflects good performance; they provide a countervailing source of bias.) In practice, avoiding survivor bias is difficult for broad-based indexes that attempt to include all hedge funds because no one knows what hedge funds exist at the current time, much less at all historical points in time. Narrow indexes are less subject to survivor bias, as are indexes that include only large hedge funds.[5]

---

[3]ZCM has constructed not only hedge fund indexes but also an actual portfolio, called the "Benchmark Series," that is intended to track the index. To avoid confusion, I use the term "benchmark" in the sense in which it is used in the rest of this monograph—a synonym for "index" when the index is being used as a point of comparison for actual portfolios. I do not follow ZCM's use of the name "Benchmark Series," in *contrast* to the index itself.

[4]Only if you envision hedge funds as operating companies (in, say, the trading and arbitrage business) does the net capital of a hedge fund represent capitalization (wealth) in the sense that we think of stocks and bonds as wealth. Even then, a hedge fund's net capital position is not a *market* price for the trading business (because it is not arrived at in an arm's-length, continuous-auction market). Its net capital position is the equivalent of a book value.

[5]For an extensive discussion of survivor bias in hedge fund indexes, see Fung and Hsieh (2002).

Rebalancing and Liquidity. Equally weighted benchmarks require frequent rebalancing, of course, to take into account ordinary changes in asset prices (net asset values in the case of hedge funds) and to reflect reconstitution (the addition or deletion of funds in the index). But rebalancing means taking money out of funds that have had the best performance to invest in others. An investor attempting to track one of these benchmarks would probably have difficulty withdrawing money from funds in the first category and might find that some of the funds in the second category were closed to new investment.

Sampling Bias. Because different methods of constructing hedge fund benchmarks result in different portfolios, returns for the same style vary substantially from one index provider to another. A particularly dramatic instance is the difference between ZCM's and EACM's equity long–short return for February 2000. ZCM reported a one-month return of +20.48 percent, whereas EACM reported –1.56 percent. In that particular month, growth stocks greatly outperformed value stocks. The ZCM benchmark was known to be growth oriented (that bias has now been eliminated); the EACM benchmark was probably value oriented.

Classifying Hedge Fund Managers into Styles. All suites of hedge fund indexes are segmented by style, but except in the case of ZCM, a manager's self-proclaimed style is used to classify the hedge fund. Instead of relying on the manager, who may have an economic interest in concealing his or her style or varying it over time, ZCM uses a statistical technique called cluster analysis to analyze each manager's historical returns and to classify the managers into styles. Any fund that does not appear to be "style pure" based on the cluster analysis is excluded from ZCM's benchmarks, which makes them exceedingly narrow (60 funds out of a possible 1,100 or so). Standard & Poor's and EACM's indexes, consisting of 40 and 100 funds, respectively, are also narrow.

Classifying hedge funds into styles has been a major source of contention among index constructors, managers, and investors. But a list of principal styles has coalesced over time as the hedge fund industry has become more focused on institutional investors as customers. The principal hedge fund styles are[6]

- convertible arbitrage,
- distressed securities,

---

[6]Note that I have avoided the popular term "relative value" because it is used as a catchall term. Virtually all long–short strategies, including all of the arbitrage styles as well as equity long–short and equity market-neutral strategies, are based on the concept of relative value. Yet, five providers of hedge fund indexes have a relative-value style index. EACM's relative-value index includes four subindexes (equity long–short, convertible arbitrage, fixed-income arbitrage, and multistrategy).

- emerging markets,
- equity long–short (long biased),
- equity market neutral,
- fixed-income arbitrage,
- global macro,
- merger and other event arbitrage, and
- short selling only.

Two styles that are structurally different from hedge funds but closely related are managed futures and funds of funds. Managed futures funds are "commodity trading advisors," not hedge funds. Funds of funds differ from hedge funds in that their only portfolio holdings are other hedge funds, not securities.

No index constructor maintains indexes for all of these styles. ZCM maintains six "style pure" style indexes and an aggregate index.

A review of the major suites of hedge fund indexes, along with a summary of the methodology for constructing each of them, is in Amenc and Martellini (2003).

Hedge Fund Factor Exposures

A number of leading researchers have pointed out that hedge fund returns, far from being unrelated to market factors, are well explained by factor exposures. Schneeweis, Kazemi, and Martin (2001) showed that up to 60 percent of the cross-sectional variation in hedge fund style benchmarks is explained by variation in the factors.

These factor exposures are somewhat different from those usually used to explain returns in traditional (long-only) portfolios, which supports the idea that hedge funds are systematically capturing risks (and, potentially, risk premiums or payoffs) that are not captured by traditional investing. Schneeweis et al. identified the following factors as having explanatory power:

- slope of the yield curve (yield difference between 30-year U.S. Treasury bond and three-month U.S. Treasury bill),
- long-term T-bond yield,
- three-month T-bill yield,
- credit spread (yield difference between Baa and Aaa bond yields),
- intramonth standard deviation of daily S&P 500 Index returns,
- S&P 500 total return,
- small-cap (Russell 2000 Index) return,
- Chicago Board Options Exchange (CBOE) Implied Volatility Index (VIX) for options on the S&P 100 Index, and
- intramonth standard deviation of daily Lehman Aggregate Bond Index.[7]

---

[7]I would add to the factor list the return difference between U.S. value and growth stocks.

Many of the factors are simply traditional asset-class exposures. Hedge funds, then, are not as much of a mystery as you might think; they are simply investment managers. Because they can sell short and use leverage, however, and because they typically operate free of a traditional asset-class benchmark, their return patterns are generally very different from those of traditional managers, and they need their own specialized benchmarks. Some benchmark constructors argue that the style-specific benchmarks capture the "natural return" of the underlying asset classes or factors and thus that the benchmarks are comparable to traditional asset-class benchmarks. If you accept this proposition, then a given hedge fund would have to add alpha relative to its style-specific benchmark to be considered successful.

Factor analyses show that hedge funds as a group are surprisingly highly correlated with the S&P 500 and sharply negatively correlated with changes in credit spreads. Merger arbitrage and other event-driven strategies are the most "short in volatility"; that is, they are negatively correlated with changes in the CBOE VIX and are thus positioned to gain from decreases in volatility and to lose when volatility increases. By and large, equity long–short funds are also short in volatility. Other categories of hedge funds are volatility neutral on average.

Hedge Fund Index Funds

If hedge funds are simply bets on pure manager skill, an investor has no reason to want an index fund of hedge funds. If hedge funds provide exposure to "priced" market factors that cannot easily be obtained through traditional investments, however, then hedge fund index funds make sense.

Unfortunately, the tracking error between a hedge fund index fund and its index is necessarily large because of the liquidity reasons noted previously. The ZCM index, however, is the basis for a series of "tracking portfolios" (deliberately not called index funds) for each of the style subindexes and for the overall index; the style-tracking portfolios typically have 2.5 percent tracking error relative to the underlying benchmarks (Amenc and Martellini).

Are Hedge Fund Indexes Peer Groups?

Anyone could be forgiven for regarding hedge fund indexes as simply peer groups, not "real" benchmarks. After all, the index constituents are portfolios (managers) and the returns are typically equally weighted, so the index return is the average of the managers' returns—which is a peer group. (In a traditional asset-class benchmark, the constituents are the underlying securities, not a set of managers.) Moreover, if you require a benchmark to be an all-inclusive, macro consistent, and (thus) cap-weighted measure of the asset class or style it is supposed to represent, hedge fund indexes do not meet those criteria.

Traditional benchmarks, however, can also be thought of as peer groups. A cap-weighted equity index (because it is the sum of all prices) represents what everybody else is holding. And if you could construct a "perfect" peer group, the cap-weighted returns of the peer group would sum to the benchmark return—because active management is a zero-sum game. With regard to any kind of market benchmark, as opposed to a so-called absolute return or liability-related benchmark, as described in Chapter 6, there is really no way out of the critique that a benchmark is a kind of peer group.

12. Policy Benchmarks

Policy benchmarks are indexes of indexes that represent the intended or normal asset mix of a plan sponsor's or investor's entire portfolio. They are used to determine whether or not, and to what extent, an investor's asset allocation and implementation (manager or security selection) are successful.

Any discussion of policy benchmarks naturally extends somewhat into the territory of investment policy itself: determining who truly owns a given asset pool, assessing its liabilities, and deciding what the asset mix should be, among other topics. My foray into this territory is limited to a few of the more pressing benchmark-related issues.

The first issue is a technical point: I extend the concept of pure alpha from Chapter 2 to the task of performance attribution at the policy or whole-plan level. The discussion then turns to some philosophical and practical issues relating to the use of policy benchmarks. While exploring those issues, I address the possibility (mentioned in previous chapters) that the *real* benchmark for investors should be their liability or intended spending.

Performance Attribution at the Policy Level

First, recall from Chapter 2 the definition of the term "active return" as (in contrast to alpha or pure alpha) the return on a portfolio minus the return on a benchmark, without any regression analyses or other adjustments for beta(s).

Brinson, Hood, and Beebower (1986) suggested that to attribute the performance of the overall investment plan as measured against a policy benchmark, you must first isolate the effect of active asset allocation against the policy benchmark, or what the authors called "timing," as follows:

Active return from asset allocation = (Actual asset weights
 × Asset-class benchmark returns)
 – Return on policy benchmark.

Then, you isolate the active return from implementation (manager selection or security selection):

Active return from implementation = (Policy weights × Actual asset-class returns)
 – Return on policy benchmark.

These parts—active return from asset allocation, active return from implementation, and the policy benchmark return itself—do not quite add up to the actual return on the portfolio. There remains a residual, or "plug" number, typically quite small, that may be regarded as coming from the interaction of asset allocation and implementation.

Potentially, a risk misfit can occur between the portfolio and the policy benchmark. If, for example, the actual asset mix was riskier than the policy mix, some of the extra return should be attributed to the higher beta rather than to the pure alpha of the active asset-allocation decisions. The market model (see Chapter 4) can be used to turn the Brinson–Hood–Beebower active return from asset allocation into a pure alpha as follows:

$$r_i = r_f + \alpha_i + \beta\,(r_m - r_f),$$

where

r_i = return given by (Policy weights × Actual asset-class returns)

r_f = riskless rate of return

α_i = pure or regression alpha of the active asset-allocation decisions versus the policy benchmark

β = beta of the return series given by (Policy weights × Actual asset-class returns), scaled so that the beta of the policy benchmark equals 1

r_m = return on the policy benchmark

A similar procedure can be followed for calculating the pure alpha added by implementation. By getting the pure alpha right, you avoid rewarding the wrong kind of behavior (such as inappropriate risk taking) and arrive at a clear measurement of the value added through active management of the asset mix.

Policy Benchmarks in Practice

Capital market theory suggests (if you accept a particularly burdensome set of assumptions) that the optimal portfolio consists of all the wealth in the world leveraged up or down to reflect a given investor's risk tolerance.[1] Most of the world's wealth is tied up in "human capital," in privately held real estate, and in private equity, but the parts that can be accessed by portfolio investors form a vast opportunity set and have been used to compose a number of different "normal portfolios" or prototypical policy benchmarks. The best known is probably Brinson Partners' Multiple Markets Index (MMI), which is constructed from the viewpoint of a U.S. investor and shown in **Table 12.1** for July 1991.

---

[1]Roll (1977) indicated why the (unobservable) cap-weighted portfolio of all risky assets in the world, not just the cap-weighted portfolio of all U.S. or all global publicly traded equities, is mean–variance efficient under the conditions of the capital asset pricing model.

Table 12.1. Brinson MMI Asset Weights, July 1991

Asset Class	Weight
Equity	
U.S. large capitalization	28%
U.S. small and mid cap	12
Other countries' equity	15
Venture capital	5
Fixed income	
U.S. investment grade	18
U.S. high yield	3
International dollar bonds	2
Nondollar bonds	5
U.S. real estate	12
Cash equivalent	0
Total	100%

Source: Brinson Partners (now part of UBS Asset Management).

Note that this allocation is not truly a "world market wealth portfolio." The weights are rigged so that equities, including venture capital but not real estate, sum to the customary 60 percent of all assets. Many categories of wealth that can be held by portfolio investors, including commodities, various types of real estate (farm land, timber, and non-U.S. real estate), and many types of private equity (buyout firms and energy partnerships), are intentionally left out. The goal of the Brinson MMI was to serve as a template for policy benchmarks, not to measure the return on the wealth of the world.[2]

Pension plan sponsors and other institutional investors in the early days of performance measurement and attribution did not reach the level of complexity represented by the MMI to determine their policy benchmarks. They more typically used something much simpler, such as

Equities	60%
Bonds	35%
Cash	5%

I will argue that the simpler approach is probably better.

---

[2]Ibbotson and Siegel (1983), updated in Ibbotson, Siegel, and Love (1985), made an explicit effort to measure the returns and weights of the global cap-weighted portfolio of all risky assets.

Simple vs. Complex Policy Benchmarks. A complex policy benchmark with many asset classes reflects the investment opportunities that exist in the world and, because it is more diversified, is more likely than a simple policy benchmark to maximize the expected return at a given level of risk. Behaviorally, however, a simple benchmark containing U.S. and international equities, bonds, inflation-linked bonds (which behave quite differently from nominal bonds), and cash has many advantages over a complex one:

- Determining the "perfect," mean–variance-efficient benchmark is too much like active management.
- Rebalancing to a complex "world wealth" benchmark that includes illiquid asset classes is costly and impractical.
- Trying to beat your benchmark is a better use of your time than perfecting the benchmark.

These points bear some elaboration. The amount of effort it takes to accomplish a task is not necessarily commensurate with the value of the work accomplished. My experience has been that asset allocation is easy and that security or manager selection is hard. Thus, the traditional 10 percent/90 percent split in effort between policy and implementation is sensible—but not because the rewards are split 10 percent/90 percent. The rewards are split in a proportion more like 40 percent/60 percent (see Ibbotson and Kaplan 2000), and getting 40 percent of the reward for 10 percent of the effort is one of the great gifts that financial markets offer to investors.

As a result, I would not put a team of experts on designing the perfectly diversified and mean–variance-optimized benchmark. Such resource deployment is better suited to active management, to beating the benchmark. In a world with limited resources, an investor should decide on a simple benchmark and spend the bulk of the resources trying to add value.

Thus, a simple approach is probably better than the MMI, although the stock/bond/cash policy benchmark is probably overdoing simplicity; a few more asset classes and a little more thought would convey some benefit.

Automatic Rebalancing vs. Use of Judgment. Some plan sponsors automatically rebalance to their policy benchmarks. The usual rationale given for such behavior is "discipline" or "contrarian investing"—buying when prices (of, say, stocks) are low and selling when they are high. This practice also is not a sound use of resources.

The benchmark is not perfect or magical. It results from an aggregation of good and bad (mostly, mediocre) estimates of expected return, risk, and correlation. Working harder on it or putting more asset classes into it (which requires more estimates) does not make it more perfect or magical. Rebalancing to a perfect portfolio would make sense, but no one knows what a perfect portfolio is.

Why not use judgment, then, to try to improve returns? A plan sponsor who feels qualified to say that this manager is better than that manager or that this stock will go up while another goes down can surely make the judgment that one asset class is more attractive than another on a relative basis at a given point in time. Asset classes are easier to analyze than stocks or managers.

The discipline that appears to result from an automatic rebalancing rule is a red herring. Automatic rebalancing is a way of falling back on fake precision. Institutions with little or no investment capability in their staff can make a sound case for automatic rebalancing, but plan sponsors who take a great deal of investment responsibility in other areas can surely take responsibility for deviating from the asset weights in a policy benchmark.

Importance of Peer Groups. Some investors take the position that they are going to disregard what other institutions are doing and simply pursue their own vision. This attitude ignores what may well be the best thinking on the topic. Some laughable examples of herd behavior in investing may exist, but in general, plan sponsors and asset owners take their responsibilities seriously and are highly capable. These professionals have as their responsibility (basically, their only responsibility) the task of thinking about what asset mix is best for their plan and then implementing it.

Thus, asset-allocation data for a plan sponsor's peer group contain real information—as do data for other peer groups and the comments and suggestions received at industry conferences and through other informal channels. To believe that you should follow your own instincts and dreams rather than respect the conclusions of generally well-informed and well-meaning peers is hubris of the worst kind. You should care greatly what other people think.

This recommendation does not mean you should not vary from the allocations of your peer group if your liability or risk tolerance is different from theirs—that is, if your peer group is improperly constructed or if, for some structural reason, your institution does not have any direct peers. You will get in real trouble, however, by thinking you don't have peers when you do.

Benchmarks and Investment Policy

Any discussion of policy benchmarks naturally drifts into a discussion of policy. In this section, I explore policy issues.[3] The guiding principle comes from Peter Bernstein's suggestion (see Chapter 6) that the real benchmark

---

[3]The issues discussed in this section will be developed further in an article in progress by the author and M. Barton Waring of Barclays Global Investors. The discussion presented here emerged from the work we have done in preparing to write that article. I thank Mr. Waring for his contribution to it.

for any asset pool is the liability of the fund or, in the absence of a legal liability, the present value of the intended spending out of the fund.[4] This discussion focuses on corporate defined-benefit (DB) pension plans, although the general principles can be applied (directly or indirectly) to any program of investing to pay liabilities or expenses over the long term, including endowments, foundations, and the savings and retirement plans of individuals.

Who Owns the Plan Assets? At first blush, the law in the United States is unambiguous on the question of what a DB pension plan assets are for. They exist to guarantee that the pension promised to beneficiaries will be paid, and the assets are to be managed for the "exclusive benefit" of those beneficiaries.[5] Superficially, pension managers are exhorted, if not required, to hold the combination of assets with risk and return characteristics that match the pension's liabilities as closely as can be accomplished.

But as everyone knows, few pensions are really managed that way. Most pension liabilities resemble a portfolio of nominal bonds and inflation-linked issues (such as U.S. Treasury Inflation-Indexed Securities, or TIPS) with a small equity component to represent, for instance, the increase over time in real incomes that results from participating in a thriving industry.[6] Most DB pension funds are invested, in contrast, roughly 60–70 percent in equities, with the remainder in fixed income, cash, and sometimes "alternative" (largely equitylike) assets, such as hedge funds and private equity. Where does this mismatch between assets and liabilities come from? Is it good or bad for beneficiaries, for the sponsor, for society?

Until about a generation ago, most pension plans were managed as though they were stand-alone financial institutions with the sole purpose of paying benefits to retirees. As such, they tended to be managed to a close match between assets and liabilities; sometimes they bought bonds, or a mix of bonds and equities, but they bought primarily annuities from insurance companies—which defease (or fund in advance) pension liabilities quite effectively if the

---

[4]The return on the "liability benchmark" is thus the rate of change of the present value of the liability or the rate of change in the present value of the intended spending out of the fund.

[5]Note that pension funds are needed only because some possibility exists that the sponsor will go bankrupt. If there were no possibility that a plan sponsor could fail to honor its obligations, a pay-as-you-go system (in which benefits are paid out of the company's or other organization's current income) would work perfectly well with no need for advance funding (investing).

[6]In addition, some of the idiosyncratic risk in a given company's pension liability cannot be modeled as either fixed income or equity risk; therefore, you cannot do anything about it (other than to make additional contributions to the fund as required).

pension benefit does not have a cost-of-living adjustment (COLA).[7] In other words, like banks and insurance companies, traditionally managed pension funds took relatively little "gap risk" (the risk that assets will move differently from liabilities). Gap risk can come from a mismatch in the equity beta, nominal interest rate duration, or real interest duration of assets and liabilities or from other sources.[8]

Dominance of Equities. If early U.S. pension plans were managed without taking much gap risk, what changed? First, high inflation rates made keeping up with the pension promise through fixed-income investing difficult. Typical pension contracts are based on "final" pay—that is, the level of pay at or around the time the employee retires. Final pay reflects salary inflation from the time the benefits are earned until the employee retires, which makes the liability sensitive to inflation even in the absence of a postretirement COLA. Second, the Employee Retirement Income Security Act of 1974 and various Financial Accounting Standards Board rulings provided an extremely complex and flexible set of funding and accounting rules for U.S. pensions that allowed sponsors to try to make a profit from their pension plans. At first, the profit could be directly channeled into the sponsor's bank account through pension plan "reversions," or payouts to the sponsor, but these reversions were later taxed so punitively that the profit could only be realized through "contribution holidays." Through these methods, sponsors tried to get the stock market (and other markets) to pay for their employees' retirement benefits for free, or at a deep discount.

---

[7]"Insured" plans actually bought annuities for their participants, so the issuing insurance company, not the sponsor, paid benefits to retirees. In contrast, in "trusteed" plans (the modern structure), the sponsor buys annuities, bonds, and other securities and pays benefits to retirees. My comment about annuities defeasing only noninflating liabilities reflects the fact that during the period when the traditional pension management methods described here were prevalent, no inflation-indexed annuities existed.

[8]The distinction between nominal and real interest rate duration, which is fully described in Siegel (2003), may be summarized as follows: The price of a T-bond that is fully inflation indexed, such as TIPS, is insensitive to changes in expected inflation because any such change is matched by an equal change in the bond's expected cash flows; the changes in the cash flows and the discount rate cancel each other out, and the price remains unchanged. Thus, TIPS have an inflation duration, or sensitivity of price with respect to changes in expected inflation, of zero. Like nominal bonds, however, TIPS are sensitive (with a negative sign) to changes in the real interest rate. This sensitivity is the real interest rate duration of TIPS. Thus, TIPS have not one but two durations. This logic implies that any set of cash flows—from a nominal bond, a pension liability, and so forth—has these two durations, although for a nominal bond, they are equal and not separately observable (because the effect of a change in a nominal bond's yield on its price is the same whether the change in yield comes from a change in expected inflation or from a change in real interest rates).

Moreover, when the Pension Benefit Guaranty Corporation (PBGC) was set up by the U.S. federal government to guarantee a minimum level of benefits to employees of bankrupt sponsors, sponsors then had a "put option" that enabled them to take more risk without forcing beneficiaries to share in all of it. They could, instead, force the other companies whose pension plans were guaranteed by the PBGC to share in the risk taking.

Treynor (1972), writing pseudonymously as "Walter Bagehot," provided a respectable grounding for the practice of taking risk to earn additional returns for the sponsor. He and many subsequent authors, building on his work, argued that the pension plan is, in effect, an operating financial subsidiary of the sponsoring corporation, and they composed an "augmented balance sheet" in which pension assets and liabilities were added to, respectively, corporate assets and liabilities to draw the true picture facing shareholders. The pension subsidiary, like any other unit of the company, was said to have the responsibility of helping the sponsor maximize its shareholders' wealth. This maximization could be done, they argued, in the context of providing beneficiaries with a guarantee of benefits by managing the assets properly. If you took additional risk—say, equity risk, which has a return expectation higher than that of the primarily fixed-income mix that most closely matches the liability—the rewards from taking that risk would flow directly to the shareholders without compromising the beneficiaries. If the risk happened not to pay off, additional contributions from the sponsor to the plan would be required to make the beneficiaries whole.[9] This wisdom began to be taught (along with much else about maximizing shareholder value) in business schools in the late 1970s and continues to be taught to this day. But what happened to sponsors who took this advice?

At first, most did extremely well. Two decades of bull markets enabled sponsors to reap large profits from their pension plans, generally by taking long contribution holidays. Some spectacular exceptions occurred, primarily when poor management of the pension plan coincided with bankruptcy of the sponsoring corporation. The PBGC was forced to take over a large number of

---

[9]This strategy, which is the basis for the modern pension system, depends on the company not entering or approaching bankruptcy (because one would not want the required pension contribution, in case risk taking in the pension plan failed to pay off, to tip the company into bankruptcy).

plans because of insolvency, but the amounts paid represented a small portion of the total dollar value of pension plans overall.[10]

Indeed, the "augmented balance sheet" view of the pension plan works well in rising markets or when companies have no capital constraint (so companies can borrow or can sell equity to meet pension shortfalls). Growing, financially healthy companies can generally operate as if they had no capital constraints, or not enough to make a difference for pension management.

▪ *The so-called pension crisis.* Markets go down as well as up, however, and companies go bankrupt or face high capital costs even though they are not bankrupt. In the bear market of 2000–2002, as in previous bear markets, pension surpluses quickly turned to shortfalls, as would be expected when stock prices decline if pension funds are exposed to equities. But this time, bonds also rallied tremendously, with lower interest rates causing pension liabilities to soar (in present value terms) at the same time that asset values were plummeting.

This entirely predictable and avoidable "crisis" did not cause universal distress. Many large companies had no DB plans or had small ones relative to the size of the company and thus were basically unaffected.[11] Severe problems arose only for a modest number of companies—primarily those in the auto, steel, airline, and a few other industries where profit growth had failed to keep pace with pension obligations—but the red flag of risk was raised for all to see. As a result, many companies "terminated" their DB plans (by buying annuities and not accepting further contributions) out of fear that the mysterious risk disease would strike them next. Few companies have started new DB plans in the aftermath of the bear market.

▪ *Lessons from the beta mismatch.* What I find surprising is that companies are apparently having such difficulty identifying the true source of their pension funds' apparent riskiness. The source of risk is, of course, the mismatch in beta, real interest rate duration, and inflation duration between

---

[10] Steven A. Kandarian, executive director of the PBGC, stated, "PBGC insures pension benefits worth $1.5 trillion and is responsible for paying current and future benefits to 783,000 people in over 3,000 terminated defined benefit plans. As a result of the recent terminations of several very large plans, PBGC will be responsible for paying benefits to nearly 1 million people in FY 2003. Similarly, benefit payments that exceeded $1.5 billion dollars in FY 2002 will rise to nearly $2.5 billion in FY 2003." But the 783,000 participants receiving current or deferred payments from the PBGC are a tiny minority of the roughly 44 million DB plan participants whose pensions are insured by that organization. See "Statement of Steven A. Kandarian, Executive Director, Pension Benefit Guaranty Corporation, before the Committee on Finance, United States Senate, March 11, 2003": www.pbgc.gov/news/speeches/Testimony031103.pdf.

[11] Their employees were, of course, affected in their defined-contribution (DC) plans by falling stock prices; virtually all companies with no DB plan have a DC plan for their employees.

the assets and the liabilities. Not only were pension plans "long" in equity beta; they were also "short" in real interest rate duration and "long" in inflation duration after netting out assets and liabilities. This mismatch can be easily fixed. Pension plans can be managed to have little risk. Such a prudent policy, which involves investing in more nominal fixed-income assets and inflation-linked assets (e.g., TIPS), may have a larger apparent cost but not a larger true cost: Companies are already implicitly paying the economic cost of underfunding, with this implied cost showing up as a shrunken share price.

Another way to look at the cost issue is by observing that the cost of making a pension promise is set by the terms of the promise, not by the means of financing it—in other words, the Modigliani and Miller (1958) invariance proposition in a slightly different guise. More precisely, the present value of the promise (liability) is the same no matter what assets are bought in an attempt to defease it. Buying assets with a higher expected return does not raise the present value of the portfolio, as should be obvious to anyone who thinks about it for a second. A dollar of high-risk, high-expected-return assets should have its future cash flows discounted back to the present at a higher rate so that it is worth the same amount as a dollar of low-risk, low-expected-return assets: it's worth a dollar. You cannot change the present value of a portfolio by changing the asset mix.

At any rate, if shareholders want to be long in equity beta, or take any other risk position, they can do it on their own at very low cost through futures or index funds. There is no compelling reason why the companies they invest in should do it for them through their pension plans. I am not saying that sponsors should not take any beta risk, only that they have good reason to rethink how much they take.

To conclude this tale, pension plans should generally be managed to pay the liabilities, not to enrich the company's shareholders. A pension manager could adopt this approach literally by holding the portfolio of assets with the lowest possible tracking error to the "liability benchmark" introduced into the discussion by Bernstein in Chapter 6. Such a portfolio would consist primarily of nominal and inflation-indexed bonds, with some equities and equitylike securities. Nothing is wrong with trying to earn a higher return than that combination, however, as long as the sponsor fully understands the risk of doing so and is in a position to take that risk without compromising the beneficiaries.

The sponsor who uses a liability benchmark and takes active risk against that benchmark by holding additional equities or other risky assets will be accounting properly for that risk if the sponsor adopts, at a conceptual level, the active risk–active return framework discussed in Chapter 2. Note that I am using the term "active risk" in a slightly different context than previously. Active risk means deviating from a benchmark, whether by selecting securities or by selecting asset-class weights different from those in the liability or policy benchmark. In other words, if you deviate from the liability benchmark by holding more equities—that is, by taking more beta risk—you are taking active risk. Active risk, in this sense, could also mean taking real interest rate risk or inflation risk relative to the liability benchmark. And each kind of active risk taken, relative to the liability benchmark, must be justified by a defensible expectation of an active return from that risk that is high enough to "pay for" the risk taken—in more technical terms, to add utility after subtracting the appropriate penalty for active risk in Equation 3.1. (Recall that in that equation, the penalty for active risk is the investor's risk aversion parameter, lambda, times the active variance, or square of active standard deviation.)

Public and Nonprofit Plans. So far, the discussion has focused on corporate pension plans, where audited and publicly available balance sheets prevail (I hope!) and the stock price is a living gauge of how well investors think the company is doing at managing the pension plan (as well as its other activities). But the principles outlined apply as well to public and nonprofit plans. Because these types of sponsors may be less sensitive to risks and costs than corporate plans, and because they are not "covered" by security analysts, public and nonprofit sponsors have tended to keep their DB plans in place, but the economic effect of gap risk is the same no matter who the bearer of the risk is. Public and nonprofit plan sponsors should also manage their plans with sensitivity to the liabilities and with an awareness of the cost of taking gap risk, which predictably will have a negative payoff in some time periods.

Individual Investors. Although the problems facing individuals saving for retirement (on their own or through a DC plan) are superficially quite different from those facing a DB plan sponsor, the ultimate goal is similar— namely, to guarantee a lifetime income to the investor.[12] (In the case of the individual, the plan is a one-person plan, so the opportunity to share risk is greatly reduced. One way individuals can share mortality risk is to buy annuities from a commercial provider.) Individuals should manage their personal portfolios as asset/liability portfolios, where the liabilities are the cash flows out of the portfolio (i.e., income) that the investor will require in retirement. Individuals have more flexibility than corporate plan sponsors because individuals can, presumably, live on less income than they were expecting and because excess assets can be spent or bequeathed. In addition, contributions are more flexible (in both directions) for the individual than for the corporate DB sponsor. But the idea of matching a liability benchmark, or trying to beat it by taking various kinds of risk, is the same.

---

[12]Muralidhar (2001) showed how the similarities between DB and DC plans can be exploited for the purpose of analyzing them and establishing investment policy and social policy.

Endowments and Foundations. Endowed institutions typically have no specific liabilities defined independently of their assets; instead, they try to keep their assets whole in real terms (or to achieve growth in the real value of their assets) while spending a relatively fixed percentage of asset value each year. For private foundations, annual spending must at least be equal to 5 percent of asset value; most other types of endowed institutions have more flexibility.

Asset/liability modeling has little to say about the management of these kinds of portfolios. Some institutions manage them as asset-only portfolios and use risk budgets to help establish the asset mix. Although "absolute return benchmarks" (say, inflation plus 5 percent) are sometimes said to represent the goal of an endowment portfolio, such pseudo-benchmarks convey almost no information and should not be used (as noted in Chapter 6). The management of endowed institution portfolios is a topic of ongoing research.

Two Benchmarks

Realistically, most plan sponsors are not going to hold the portfolio that minimizes tracking error to the liability benchmark. Nominal fixed-income assets and TIPS have yields that are too low for most sponsors to accept. They may not continue to hold their current average of 60–70 percent in equities, but they may hold a mix of asset classes that is quite different from the asset mix that most closely matches the liability benchmark. How should their performance be measured—using two benchmarks?

Yes.

On one side, the investor will be managing in relation to a policy benchmark in the traditional sense. For many types of asset pools, this benchmark should be more conservative and less dominated by equities than has been the practice in the last decade or so, but it will still be a policy benchmark, one that is composed of asset classes that could, if desired, be held passively through index funds. Such an investable benchmark has the measurement power that has been the focus throughout this monograph. Once the proper risk level and the policy benchmark have been determined, the investor must demonstrate that he or she has added pure alpha by deviating from the benchmark while controlling the pure active risk inherent in those deviations. On the other side, the investor will be keeping an eye on a liability-focused benchmark. A benchmark of this kind is less a passive portfolio that you could hold in the absence of active views and more a conceptual reference point for focusing the mind on the real purpose of the asset pool and on the question of whether departing from the asset mix that most closely matches this benchmark is worth the risk (based on the risk aversion the investor has to this particular kind of risk).

The real purpose of the asset pool, of course, is to pay pension benefits, to fund the operations of a foundation or endowed institution, or to provide for the living expenses of an individual saver. By forcing investors to concentrate on the real problem at hand, a liability-focused benchmark can help them with the most crucial problem in investing—taking the right amount and right kind of risk in pursuit of the goal that they are charged with seeking.

References

Amenc, Noël, and Lionel Martellini. 2003. "The Brave New World of Hedge Fund Indices." Working paper. Available online at www.rcf.usc.edu/~martelli/papers/bnwhfi.pdf.

Arnott, Robert D., and Max Darnell. 2003. "Active versus Passive Management: Framing the Decision." *Journal of Investing*, vol. 12, no. 1 (Spring):31–36.

Asness, Clifford S., Jacques A. Friedman, Robert J. Krail, and John M. Liew. 2000. "Style Timing: Value versus Growth." *Journal of Portfolio Management*, vol. 26, no. 3 (Spring):50–60.

Ball, Ray. 1978. "Anomalies in Relationships between Securities' Yields and Yield-Surrogates." *Journal of Financial Economics,* vol. 6, nos. 2/3 (June):103–126.

Banz, Rolf W. 1981. "The Relationship between Return and Market Value of Common Stocks." *Journal of Financial Economics*, vol. 9, no. 1 (March):3–18.

Barro, Robert J. 1974. "Are Government Bonds Net Wealth?" *Journal of Political Economy,* vol. 82, no. 6 (November/December):1095–1117.

Basu, Sanjoy. 1977. "Investment Performance of Common Stocks in Relation to their Price–Earnings Ratios: A Test of the Efficient Market Hypothesis." *Journal of Finance*, vol. 32, no. 3 (June):663–681.

———. 1983. "The Relationship between Earnings Yield, Market Value, and Return for NYSE Common Stocks: Further Evidence." *Journal of Financial Economics*, vol. 12, no. 1 (June):129–156.

Bergstrom, Gary P. 1975. "A New Route to Higher Return and Lower Risk." *Journal of Portfolio Management,* vol. 2, no. 1 (Autumn):30–38.

Bernstein, Peter L. 1992. *Capital Ideas: The Improbable Origins of Modern Wall Street*. New York: Free Press.

———. 1994. "Measuring the Performance of Performance Measurement." *Economics & Portfolio Strategy*. New York: Peter L. Bernstein, Inc. (1 December).

———. 1996. *Against the Gods: The Remarkable Story of Risk*. New York: John Wiley & Sons.

———. 2000. "A Modest Proposal: Portfolio Management Practice for Modern Times." *Economics & Portfolio Strategy*. New York: Peter L. Bernstein, Inc. (15 April).

Brinson, Gary P., L. Randolph Hood, and Gilbert L. Beebower. 1986. "Determinants of Portfolio Performance." *Financial Analysts Journal*, vol. 42, no. 4 (July/August):39–44. Reprinted in *FAJ*'s 50th Anniversary Issue, vol. 51, no. 1 (January/February 1995):133–138.

Buetow, Gerald W., Jr., Robert R. Johnson, and David E. Runkle. 2000. "The Inconsistency of Returns-Based Style Analysis." *Journal of Portfolio Management*, vol. 26, no. 3 (Spring):61–77.

Clifford, Scott W., Kenneth F. Kroner, and Laurence B. Siegel. 2001. "In Pursuit of Performance: The Greatest Return Stories Ever Told," *Investment Insights,* vol. 4, no. 1 (August). San Francisco, CA: Barclays Global Investors.

Clothier, Eric, M. Barton Waring, and Laurence B. Siegel. 1998. "Is Small-Cap Investing Worth It? Two Decades of Research on Small-Cap Stocks." *Investment Insights*, vol. 1, no. 5 (December). San Francisco, CA: Barclays Global Investors.

Cowles, Alfred. 1938 (2nd ed. 1939). *Common Stock Indexes: 1871–1937.* Bloomington, IN: Principia.

Dimson, Elroy, Paul Marsh, and Mike Staunton. 2002. *Triumph of the Optimists*. Princeton, NJ: Princeton University Press.

Dynkin, Lev, Jay Hyman, and Vadim Konstantinovsky. 2002. "Sufficient Diversification in Credit Portfolios." *Journal of Portfolio Management*, vol. 29, no. 1 (Fall):89–114.

Enderle, Francis, Brad Pope, and Laurence B. Siegel. 2002. "Broad-Capitalization Indexes of the U.S. Equity Market." *Investment Insights,* vol. 5, no. 2 (May). San Francisco, CA: Barclays Global Investors.

———. 2003. "Broad-Capitalization Indexes of the U.S. Equity Market." *Journal of Investing*, vol. 12, no. 1 (Spring):11–22.

Fama, Eugene F., and Kenneth R. French. 1992. "The Cross-Section of Expected Stock Returns." *Journal of Finance,* vol. 47, no. 2 (June):427–465.

———. 1993. "Common Risk Factors in the Returns on Stocks and Bonds." *Journal of Financial Economics,* vol. 33, no. 1 (February):3–56.

Fisher, Lawrence. 1966. "An Algorithm for Finding Exact Rates of Return." *Journal of Business*, vol. 39, no. 1, part 2 (January):111–118.

Fisher, Philip A. 1958 (Anthology edition 1996). *Common Stocks and Uncommon Profits*. New York: John Wiley & Sons.

Fung, William, and David A. Hsieh. 2002. "Hedge-Fund Benchmarks: Information Content and Biases." *Financial Analysts Journal,* vol. 58, no. 1 (January/February):22–34.

Goetzmann, William N., and Mark Garry. 1986. "Does Delisting from the S&P 500 Affect Stock Price?" *Financial Analysts Journal*, vol. 42, no. 2 (March/April):64–69.

Gordon, Myron J., and Eli Shapiro. 1956. "Capital Equipment Analysis: The Required Rate of Profit." *Management Science,* vol. 3 (October):102–110.

Graham, Benjamin F., and David L. Dodd. 1934 (4th ed. 1972). *Security Analysis.* New York: McGraw-Hill.

Graham, Benjamin, and Jason Zweig. 2003. *The Intelligent Investor.* New York: HarperCollins.

Grinold, Richard C. 1989. "The Fundamental Law of Active Management." *Journal of Portfolio Management,* vol. 15, no. 3 (Spring):30–37.

———. 1990. "The Sponsor's View of Risk." In *Pension Fund Investment Management: A Handbook for Investors and Their Advisors.* Edited by Frank J. Fabozzi. Chicago, IL: Probus.

Grinold, Richard C., and Ronald N. Kahn. 2000. 2nd ed. *Active Portfolio Management.* New York: McGraw-Hill.

Grossman, Sanford J., and Joseph E. Stiglitz. 1980. "On the Impossibility of Informationally Efficient Markets." *American Economic Review*, vol. 70, no. 3 (June):393–408.

Harris, Lawrence, and Eitan Gurel. 1986. "Price and Volume Effects Associated with Changes in the S&P 500 List: New Evidence for the Existence of Price Pressures." *Journal of Finance,* vol. 41, no. 4 (September):815–829.

Haugen, Robert A. 1995. *The New Finance: The Case against Efficient Markets.* Englewood Cliffs, NJ: Prentice-Hall.

Ibbotson Associates. 2003. *Stocks, Bonds, Bills, and Inflation: 2003 Yearbook.* Chicago, IL: Ibbotson Associates (updates work by Roger G. Ibbotson and Rex A. Sinquefield).

Ibbotson, Roger G., and Gary P. Brinson. 1987. *Investment Markets: Gaining the Performance Advantage.* New York: McGraw-Hill.

Ibbotson, Roger G., and Paul D. Kaplan. 2000. "Does Asset Allocation Policy Explain 40, 90, or 100 Percent of Performance?" *Financial Analysts Journal*, vol. 56, no. 1 (January/February):26–33.

Ibbotson, Roger G., and Laurence B. Siegel. 1983. "The World Market Wealth Portfolio." *Journal of Portfolio Management*, vol. 9, no. 2 (Winter):5–17.

Ibbotson, Roger G., Paul D. Kaplan, and James D. Peterson. 1997. "Estimates of Small Stock Betas Are Much Too Low." *Journal of Portfolio Management*, vol. 24, no. 2 (Summer):104–111.

Ibbotson, Roger G., Laurence B. Siegel, and Kathryn S. Love. 1985. "World Wealth: Market Values and Returns." *Journal of Portfolio Management*, vol. 12, no. 1 (Fall):4–23.

Jacques, William E. 1988. "The S&P 500 Membership Anomaly, or Would You Join This Club?" *Financial Analysts Journal*, vol. 44, no. 6 (November/December):73–75.

Jain, Prem C. 1987. "The Effect on Stock Price of Inclusion in or Exclusion from the S&P 500." *Financial Analysts Journal*, vol. 43, no. 1 (January/February):58–65.

Jegadeesh, Narasimhan. 1990. "Evidence of Predictable Behavior of Security Returns." *Journal of Finance*, vol. 45, no. 3 (July):881–898.

Jensen, Michael C. 1968. "Problems in Selection of Security Portfolios: The Performance of Mutual Funds in the Period 1945–1964." *Journal of Finance*, vol. 23, no. 2 (March):389–416.

Jobson, J.D., and Bob Korkie. 1981. "Putting Markowitz Theory to Work." *Journal of Portfolio Management*, vol. 7, no. 4 (Summer):70–74.

Johnson, Stephen M., and Laurence B. Siegel. 2003. "Credit Market Volatility and Change." *Journal of Investing*, vol. 12, no. 1 (Spring):37–46.

Kahn, Ronald N. 2000. "Most Pension Plans Need More Enhanced Indexing." In *Enhanced Indexing: New Strategies and Techniques for Investors*. Edited by Brian R. Bruce. New York: Institutional Investor.

Kritzman, Mark. 1998. "Wrong and Alone." *Economics & Portfolio Strategy*. New York: Peter L. Bernstein, Inc. (15 January).

———. 2003. "Value In—Garbage Out." *Economics & Portfolio Strategy*. New York: Peter L. Bernstein, Inc. (15 January).

Kuhn, Thomas S. 1996. *The Structure of Scientific Revolutions*. 3rd ed. Chicago, IL: University of Chicago Press.

Leibowitz, Martin L., and Roy D. Henriksson. 1989. "Portfolio Optimization with Shortfall Constraints: A Confidence-Limit Approach to Managing Downside Risk." *Financial Analysts Journal*, vol. 45, no. 2 (March/April):34–41.

Lowenstein, Roger. 2001. "Value Vindicated." *SmartMoney* (August).

Madhavan, Ananth. 2002. "Index Reconstitution and Equity Returns." Unpublished manuscript. (Available online at www.itginc.com/research/whitepapers/madhavan/RusselStudy.pdf.)

Markowitz, Harry M. 1952. "Portfolio Selection." *Journal of Finance* (March):77–91.

———. 1991. *Portfolio Selection: Efficient Diversification of Investments*. 2nd. ed. Oxford, U.K.: Basil Blackwell.

Michaud, Richard. 2001. *Efficient Asset Management: A Practical Guide to Stock Portfolio Optimization and Asset Allocation*. New York: Oxford University Press. First published in 1998 by Cambridge, MA: Harvard Business School Press.

———. 2003. "An Introduction to Resampled Efficiency." *The Monitor*, Investment Management Consultants Association, vol. 18, no. 1 (January/February):22–23.

Michaud, Richard, and Robert Michaud. 2003. "Resampled Efficiency Issues." (Available online at www.newfrontieradvisors.com/downloads/pdfs/nfa-written/resampled-efficiency-issues-020103.pdf.)

Mishkin, Frederic. 1980. "Is the Preferred-Habitat Model of the Term Structure Inconsistent with Financial Market Efficiency?" *Journal of Political Economy,* vol. 88, no. 2 (April):406–411.

Modigliani, Franco, and Merton H. Miller. 1958. "The Cost of Capital, Corporation Finance, and the Theory of Investment." *American Economic Review,* vol. 48 (June):261–297.

Modigliani, Franco, and Richard Sutch. 1969. "The Term Structure of Interest Rates: A Re-Examination of the Evidence." *Journal of Money, Credit and Banking,* vol. 1, no. 1 (February):112–120.

Muralidhar, Arun S. 2001. *Innovations in Pension Fund Management*. Stanford, CA: Stanford University Press.

Newton, Isaac. 1664–1671. *De Methodus Fluxionum et Serierum Infinitorum*. London, U.K.

Phillips, Don, and Paul Kaplan. 2003. "What Comes Next? The Case for a New Generation of Indexes." *Journal of Indexes* (First quarter). (Available online at www.indexes.morningstar.com/Index/PDF/WhitePaper1.pdf.)

Pope, Brad, Chad Rakvin, and Gardner Platt. 2003. "Style Indexes of the US Equity Market." *Investment Insights,* vol. 6, no. 3 (July). San Francisco, CA: Barclays Global Investors.

Raphson, Joseph. 1690. *Analysis Aequationum Universalis.* London, U.K.

Rattray, Sandy, and Pravin Manglani. 2003. "Is Standard and Poor's Adding Return by Managing the S&P 500 Index?" Goldman Sachs Derivatives and Trading Research (27 January).

Reinganum, Marc R. 1981. "Misspecification of Capital Asset Pricing: Empirical Anomalies Based on Earnings Yields and Market Values." *Journal of Financial Economics,* vol. 9, no. 1 (March):19–46.

Roll, Richard. 1977. "A Critique of the Asset Pricing Theory's Tests." *Journal of Financial Economics*, vol. 4 (March):129–176.

Rosenberg, Barr. 1974. "Extra-Market Components of Covariance in Security Markets." *Journal of Financial and Quantitative Analysis* (March):263–274.

Rosenberg, Barr, and Vinay Marathe. 1975. "The Prediction of Investment Risk: Systematic and Residual Risk." In *Proceedings of the Seminar on the Analysis of Security Prices.* Chicago, IL: University of Chicago:85–226.

Rosenberg, Barr, Kenneth Reid, and Ronald Lanstein. 1985. "Persuasive Evidence of Market Inefficiency." *Journal of Portfolio Management*, vol. 11 (Spring):9–17.

Schneeweis, Thomas, Hossein Kazemi, and George Martin. 2001. "Understanding Hedge Fund Performance: Research Results and Rules of Thumb for the Institutional Investor." Working paper, Center for International Securities and Derivatives Markets, University of Massachusetts, Amherst (November). (Available online at www.colepartners.com/downloads/UnderstandingHedgeFundPerformance.pdf.)

Schoenfeld, Steven, and Robert Ginis. 2002. "International Equity Benchmarks for U.S. Investors." *Investment Insights,* vol. 5, no. 4 (November). San Francisco, CA: Barclays Global Investors.

Sharpe, William F. 1964. "Capital Asset Prices: A Theory of Market Equilibrium under Conditions of Risk." *Journal of Finance*, vol. 19, no. 3 (September): 425–442.

———. 1970. *Portfolio Theory and Capital Markets.* Reprint ed. 2000. New York: McGraw-Hill.

———. 1988. "Determining a Fund's Effective Asset Mix." *Investment Management Review,* vol. 2, no. 6 (November/December):59–69.

————. 1992. "Asset Allocation: Management Style and Performance Measurement." *Journal of Portfolio Management*, vol. 18, no. 2 (Winter):7–19.

Sharpe, William F., Gordon J. Alexander, and Jeffery V. Bailey. 1995. *Investments*. 5th ed. Englewood Cliffs, NJ: Prentice-Hall.

Shefrin, Hersh. 2001. "Do Investors Expect Higher Returns from Safer Stocks than from Riskier Stocks?" *Journal of Psychology and Financial Markets*, vol. 2, no. 4 (December):176–181.

————. 2002. *Beyond Greed and Fear*. New York: Oxford University Press.

Siegel, Laurence B. 2003. "TIPS, the Double Duration, and the Pension Plan." Presented at the Barclays Capital Global Inflation-Linked Bond Conference, Key Biscayne, FL (January). A revised version, co-authored with M. Barton Waring, is forthcoming in the *Financial Analysts Journal*.

Siegel, Laurence B., Kenneth F. Kroner, and Scott W. Clifford. 2001. "The Greatest Return Stories Ever Told." *Journal of Investing*, vol. 10, no. 2 (Summer): 91–102.

Sikorsky, Nilly. 1982. "The Origin and Construction of the Capital International Indices." *Columbia Journal of World Business*, vol. 17 (Summer):24–41.

Solnik. Bruno. 1974. "Why Not Diversify Internationally?" *Financial Analysts Journal,* vol. 30, no. 4 (July/August):48–53.

Sortino, Frank A., and Stephen E. Satchell. 2001. *Managing Downside Risk in Financial Markets*. Oxford, U.K.: Butterworth-Heinemann.

Thomas, Landon, Jr. 1999. "Confessions of a Fund Manager." *SmartMoney* (April). (Available online at www.smartmoney.com/10/index.cfm?Story= feature-confessions.)

Treynor, Jack L. (Using pseudonym Walter Bagehot). 1972. "Risk and Reward in Corporate Pension Funds." *Financial Analysts Journal* (January/February): 80–84.

Waring, M. Barton, and Laurence B. Siegel. 2003. "The Dimensions of Active Management." *Journal of Portfolio Management*, vol. 29, no. 3 (Spring):35–51. (Available online at www.iijpm.com/common/getArticle.asp?ArticleID=18465.)

Waring, M. Barton, John Pirone, Duane Whitney, and Charles Castille. 2000. "Optimizing Manager Structure and Budgeting Manager Risk." *Journal of Portfolio Management*, vol. 25, no. 3 (Spring):90–104. (Available online at www.iijpm.com/jlevypdfs/2-4.pdf.)

Williams, John Burr. 1956. *The Theory of Investment Value*. Amsterdam, Netherlands: North-Holland. Originally published in 1938 by Cambridge, MA: Harvard University Press.

Selected AIMR Publications

Benchmarks and Attribution Analysis, 2001

Best Execution and Portfolio Performance, 2001

Closing the Gap between Financial Reporting and Reality, 2003

Core-Plus Bond Management, 2001

Developments in Quantitative Investment Models, 2001

Equity Portfolio Construction, 2002

Equity Research and Valuation Techniques, 2002

Equity Valuation in a Global Context, 2003

Ethical Issues for Today's Firm, 2000

Evolution in Equity Markets: Focus on Asia, 2001

Fixed-Income Management: Credit, Covenants, and Core-Plus, 2003

Fixed-Income Management for the 21st Century, 2002

Hedge Fund Management, 2002

Investment Counseling for Private Clients IV, 2002

Investment Firms: Trends and Issues, 2001

Managing Today's Investment Firm, 2003

Organizational Challenges for Investment Firms, 2002

A full catalog of publications is available on AIMR's World Wide Web site at **www.aimr.org**. You may write to AIMR, P.O. Box 3668, Charlottesville, VA 22903 U.S.A.; call 434-951-5499; fax 434-951-5262; or e-mail **info@aimr.org** to receive a free copy of our product catalog. All prices are subject to change.